some marginal
ink marking

KU-466-791

B//   127751

THE
DAYS OF THE FATHERS
IN ROSS-SHIRE

JOHN KENNEDY

CHRISTIAN FOCUS PUBLICATIONS

The Days of the Fathers
in Ross-shire.
First published 1861

This edition published by
Christian Focus Publications
Henderson Road, Inverness IV1 1SP
© June 1979

ISBN 0 906731 00 3

Printed in Great Britain by
Bookmag, Henderson Road, Inverness IV1 1SP

CONTENTS

6 CONTENTS

CHAPTER 4

THE RELIGION OF ROSS-SHIRE

CHAPTER 4

THE RELIGION OF ROSS-SHIRE

Page

CHAPTER 4 *Page*

John Kennedy, D.D.

BIOGRAPHICAL INTRODUCTION

With a heavy heart, a Highland minister made the following entry in his diary, almost a hundred years ago: 'My beloved friend and nearest brother-minister, Dr Kennedy of Dingwall, died at Bridge of Allan, on Monday, 28th April 1884. The desolation of his bereavement cannot be recorded. Not only are his beloved wife and daughter stricken and prostrate, but the whole Highlands mourn'. That profound grief was seen, for instance, on the day that Dr Kennedy's remains arrived at Dingwall Station from Bridge of Allan, when, as one observer noted, 'tears flowed copiously' among the waiting crowd.

Who then was this man, once so loved? His life may be summarised as follows:

1819, born in Killearnan, Ross-shire, the fourth son of the saintly Rev. John Kennedy;

1843, completed his studies in Aberdeen and was licensed to preach the gospel by the Presbytery of Chanonry;

1844, ordained and inducted to the pastorate of Dingwall Free Church congregation;

1848, married to Mary MacKenzie, daughter of Major Forbes MacKenzie of Fodderty;

1861, publication of his first book, *The Days of the Fathers in Ross-shire*;

1873, degree of D.D. conferred on him by Aberdeen University;

1884, died at Bridge of Allan, on his way home from a convalescent holiday in Italy.

The life so tersely summarised was no ordinary life. It was, in fact, a life of unstinted and faithful service to Christ, by one who was both great in godliness and greatly gifted.

A life of Christian service must be preceded by the spiritual
renovation of the individual; but young John Kennedy, although
studying for the ministry, was a stranger to that fundamental
change and was quite careless about his soul. Then, one day, he was
given the devasting news of his father's death. Crushed to the core
and full of grief, he hurried home on a cold January morning in
1841. That bitter bereavement proved to be, by God's blessing, the
turning point of his life. Deeply realising, for the first time, his need
of salvation, he began earnestly to seek for it and was enabled to
believe in Christ, as he said to a friend, ''with a faith which,
although weak in degree, was saving in nature''. A truly transformed John Kennedy returned to college to complete his studies.

While not yet 25, he became the first minister of the Free Church
congregation in Dingwall. Such was his popularity that many other
congregations, including an Australian one, invited him to be their
pastor, but he remained in Dingwall until his death 40 years later.
His work was not confined to Dingwall however. Congregations all
over the Highlands and in other parts of Scotland highly esteemed
him as a preacher of almost unequalled power. In fact, his
biographers, and others who were able to judge, united in regarding
him as the most outstanding preacher of his generation in the
Highlands.

His manner in the pulpit was strikingly impressive. The editor of
The British Weekly wrote: 'He at once fascinated us by the
arresting solemnity of his manner and the spring-like newness of his
English'. Another editor, James Barron of *The Inverness Courier*,
described his appearance as: 'not tall, but handsome, strongly
built, supple and yet stately . . . His features were pleasant and firm,
suggesting both strength and tenderness'. Barron, who had heard
most of the great national speakers of the day, considered that 'for
sheer power over an audience, there was none to surpass Dr
Kennedy at his best'.

The content of his preaching was predominantly 'Jesus Christ
and Him crucified'. The sinners need of Christ was made starkly
clear as he faithfully declared the claims of God's law and as he
skilfully unveiled the depravity of the human heart and the awful

nature of sin. In proceeding to demonstrate the glory of Christ as the great and only Saviour and in earnestly commending Him to the acceptance of sinners, 'his utterances', wrote Noble, 'assumed their greatest power . . . Christ was the centre and sun of his preaching'.

His preaching was blessed to many. One man, burdened by sin, walked many miles to hear Dr Kennedy and said later, ''He showed me all my heart and into its bleeding wound he poured the oil of consolation''. A Stornoway hearer testified, ''The manifestations I had that day of the glorious majesty, worthiness and suitableness of the Lord Jesus Christ in all His mediatorial offices I never experienced before nor indeed to the same extent since. I can never forget it''.

Then there was the feeding of the Lord's people; a work in which Dr Kennedy was greatly experienced. An old Christian in Caithness declared, ''Mr Kennedy above others is a means of warming my cold heart and reviving something of the love of days gone by''. A Dundee man wrote to Dr Kennedy: 'I desire to bless God for having heard you . . . Your sermon on the electing love of God was a seasonable message to my soul, clearing difficulties and confirming me in the truth'.

While Dr Kennedy was so highly regarded throughout the country he was loved especially by his own people in Dingwall. They set a high premium on his preaching but they also valued his pastoral visits, particulary at times of sickness and bereavement, when his tender sympathy for them was so evident. The young people of the congregation well knew the affectionate and practical interest which he had in them, while the poor in the congregation had experience of what the 1884 Assembly described as 'his large-hearted liberality'. 'Dr Kennedy was never rich', wrote Norman MacFarlane, 'and he had the art of constantly making himself poor'. When he was remonstrated with on one occasion for being generous to a fault he cheerfully replied, ''Freely ye have received, freely give''.

There were others, besides those in particular need, who greatly appreciated his friendship. C. H. Spurgeon, for example, spoke of him as 'wonderfully tender and sympathetic'; and when he went

North to preach at the opening of Dr Kennedy's new church, he regarded the short stay which he had with Dr Kennedy as a 'sunny spot' in his life. The Dingwall manse was renowned for its warm hospitality and Dr Kennedy's 'loving nature', as one visitor noted, 'instilled happiness all round'. His vivacious and gentle wife was not a whit behind in generosity and their unity of mind and action indicated to another visitor that 'both alike shared deeply the same great faith in the unstinting liberality of God's providence'.

Dr Kennedy, however, could be as firm as he was amiable. 'This gentle loving humble man', wrote Dr McEwan, 'stood like the rocks of his native mountains when questions of principle were at stake'. He held firmly the Establishment principle and therefore vigorously opposed the projected union of the Free Church with the United Presbyterian Church — a church which rejected the civil establishment of religion as 'injurious' and unscriptural; and again, in the 1873 Assembly, he seconded Dr Begg's motion against disestablishment with strong and lucid arguments. The Regulative principle was dear to him also, as was shown by his determined resistance to the proposed introduction of uninspired hymns and instrumental music to the public worship of God.

The growing signs of deviation from Reformed doctrine alarmed him most. With regard to those who pled for the modifying and abolishing of creeds he said, ''Confessions to them are troublesome things, not because they interpose between them and Scripture but because they show when they depart from it''. He also deplored a presentation of the gospel which ignored or belittled 'the sovereignty and power of God in the dispensation of His grace', and for this reason, among others, he criticised the revival movement of the day, in his pamphlet, *Hyper-Evangelism,* (1874). As a result, some charged him with Hyper-Calvinism, but 'no man in his generation', wrote Dr MacLeod in his *Scottish Theology,* 'made conscience more than he did of proclaiming as the Gospel a message that was as full as it was free and as free as it was full'.

It was his heralding of this full and free message which endeared him to the hearts of the people, as an eminently distinguished ambassador of the cross. When, therefore, his health markedly deteriorated in the winter of 1883 his many friends prayed fervently that the prescribed holiday in a milder climate would restore him. But that was not to be. The news of his death, in the spring of 1884, came as a stunning blow and cast a gloom over the North. As the Assembly of that year recorded in its minutes, 'Since the death of Dr MacDonald of Ferintosh, the Apostle of the North, no death caused deeper sorrow throughout the Highlands than that of Dr John Kennedy of Dingwall'.

What Dr Kennedy left in writing was comparatively limited because of the incessantly busy life which he had led. In addition to his three books, *The Days of the Fathers in Ross-shire*, *The Apostle of the North* and *Man's Relation to God*, he wrote about a dozen pamphlets and booklets. His aim in writing *The Days of the Fathers in Ross-shire* was to preserve the memory of the godly ministers and men of Ross-shire at a time when, as he wrote in the preface, 'lifeless formality was taking the place of their godliness'. In the preface to the second edition he wrote: 'I expected that many would count me credulous and some call me superstitious and a few denounce me as fanatical, because of some anecdotes I gave, to prove how near to God were the godly of former days'. The anecdotes he referred to gave instances of intimations of God's will being secretly impressed upon the minds of certain godly persons. These 'higher attainments of the godly', he explained, were nothing more than 'the operation of the Spirit on the soul and the seasonable presentation and application of the truth'. He expanded this explanation in his sermon on, 'The secret of the Lord is with them that fear him', Psa. 25.14, which is included in this edition. While there were some people who criticised *The Days of the Fathers in Ross-shire*, as he anticipated, there were others — many others in this country and abroad — by whom his book was warmly welcomed and read with delight.

This new edition consists only of the material contained in the fourth edition, the last edition published during Dr Kennedy's life, and therefore omits the biographies of Dr Kennedy and of his wife which were added to later editions and also omits the prefaces of previous editions. This biographical introduction attempts to replace these omissions.

The publishers send out this edition with the prayer that, by the Divine blessing, it may be conducive to the reviving and fostering of that vital godliness which it vividly portrays.

NEIL M. ROSS,
Ullapool,
Ross-shire,
13th April 1979.

The Days of the Fathers
in Ross-shire

CHAPTER I

THE GOSPEL IN ROSS-SHIRE

WILD and uncultivated as their native hills, were the people of the north when already, in some parts of the Lowlands, the desert was beginning to "rejoice and blossom as the rose." The winter of the north had lasted long, and dark and dreary had it been throughout. And when "the time to favour" — "the set time" — had come, protracted and broken was the work of spring; but a genial summer followed, and a rich harvest was thereafter gathered. Cold and dreary, or dark and stormy, may be the winter that shall close this year of "visitation." The chill of its presence is already on the hearts of "the living"; but who can tell, whether it shall continue to advance with the quiet of a blight, or yet burst upon us with the fury of a tempest?

When the Gospel was first sent to the Highlands, Popery claimed the whole region as its own, although its dogmas were not generally known, nor its rites universally practised. Fearing no competing religion, the priesthood had been content to rule the people, without attempting to teach them. His ignorance and superstition made the rude Highlander all the more manageable in the hands of the clergy, and they, therefore, carefully kept him a heathen. He believed that the priests were as powerful as the fairies, and he brought venison to the bishop, and thus rendered her due of faith and of practice to the Church. In exchange there was given him all the wild license which he craved. Popery has always had an easy way of making conquests in heathendom. If it can only steal in its baptism among the rites formerly practised, and hang a crucifix on every idol formerly worshipped, and attract to its priesthood the blind veneration of the people, it will consent to leave all else as it

found it. Such must have been its conquest of the Highlands of
Scotland. Savage heathen could everywhere be found, trained Papists
in very few places, when the light of the Gospel first shone on the
north. There was even then quite as much of what was peculiar to
Druidism, in the religious opinions and worship of the people, as of
any views and practices derived from Popery.

There were then in the Highlands, clans, each with its chief, as
well as congregations, each with its priest. The influence of the
castle had never been displaced by that of the chapel, anxious
though the Romish hierarchy ever were for a monopoly of power.
Had the clergy attempted to supersede the chieftains, they would
have assumed the attitude of rivals before them, and on this the
Highlanders had never learned to look without being provoked to a
trial of strength. Had they even endeavoured to check them, they
might have become unmanageable. They, therefore, wisely gave
them rein, careful only to direct them; for, having learned to
manage, they cared not to remove them. Their power having been
made useful to the Church, the priests were rather anxious to
preserve it. Each found it his interest to acknowledge and advance
the influence of the other. The chief sent his clansman, with blood
on his hands, for peace to the priest; and the more guilty the
devotee had become in the service of the former, his fear made
him all the more servile in the hands of the latter. The priest sent
his penitent, with an indulgence, to the service of the chief; and the
more the serf placed his trust in the power of the Church, all the
more boldly could he fight the future battles of his clan. The clergy,
too, must themselves, be Celts; and as no way had been found of
emptying his veins of Highland blood, while leaving him fit for
Highland service, the clannish feeling was strong even in the priest.
He could be moved, sometimes, to subordinate the claims of his
chief at Rome to the wishes of his chief at home. Priest Mackenzie
could be persuaded to gather the Macleods or the Munros to mass
at an appointed time, that his chieftain might find it convenient to
butcher or to burn them. A levy from the clan would be the
churchman's reward for this service. The two thus helped each
other; and, combined, they bore with the pressure of a double

despotism on the deluded people, the chieftain using all his influence to keep them serfs and savages, and the priest doing his utmost to keep them dupes and fanatics. Alas! for the poor Highlander under them. He, with an energy and ardour that made him a hero, even when a slave, and a love of country and of kindred that made him a patriot, even when oppressed, was found by the Reformation as Popery had left him, an utter heathen in ignorance, a very fanatic in superstition, and, in his habits, a lawless savage, rioting in the wild excitements of the chase, in the perilous adventures of plundering raids, and in the fierce combats of rival clans and chieftains.

It was in 1563 the first ray of Reformation light broke through the darkness of Ross-shire. By the General Assembly of that year, Mr Donald Munro was appointed "Commissioner of Ross." The Lord came with him to his work, and before seven years had passed, the cause of truth had made such progress in Easter Ross, where he chiefly laboured, as to attract the notice of the "good Regent Murray," who presented to the people of Tain a pulpit for their church, as an acknowledgment of their zeal.

In 1574 ten ministers and twenty-five readers were labouring in Ross-shire. The county was divided into ten districts, each containing several charges. To each district a minister was appointed, and, so far as the supply afforded, a reader to each charge. The several congregations in his district were visited by the minister, though he had the immediate oversight of the charge which was accounted the central or the most important. This arrangement was, of course, only temporary, and was gradually abandoned, as the supply of ministers was increasing. Efficient readers it was difficult to procure, and a number adequate for the supplying of all the charges it was quite impossible to find. It was difficult, too, to confine such as were employed to the work which alone was assigned to them. Some of them had formerly been priests, and while required only to read to the people, they could not be kept from going beyond their commission into the track of their old course of service. The ministers, too, were liable to prelatic aspirations, and it was well, for themselves and for others, that the temptation to lord it over subordinate labourers was removed, so soon as the Church could displace, by an ordained pastorate, the temporary office of the readers. Of the work and success of the labourers in Ross-shire, during the sixteenth century, no distinct memories have survived.

Little is known of the state of matters in Ross-shire during the days of the Tulchans. The Bishop of Ross, who was deposed by the Assembly of 1638, was one who was likely to use all his influence in suppressing the truth, and in oppressing the people who loved it. On the occasion of his deposition, Mr Alexander Kerse said, "He is the vive example and perfyte paterne of a proud prelat, and enters in composition with the Pope himselfe; and, therefore, let him have his due deposition and excommunication"; "and the whole Assembly, in ane voice, voited the same."

On the re-establishment of Presbytery, after the days of the Tulchans, the people were found to be still grossly ignorant and superstitious, and the state of morals to be extremely low. During a visitation of the more remote Highland parishes in 1656, the Presbytery of Dingwall found that "amongst their abominable and heathenish practices, the people (of Applecross) were accustomed to sacrifice bulls at a certaine time, upon the 25th of August, which day is dedicate, as they conceive, to S. Mourie, as they call him." Whether this Mourie was a heathen deity, or a Popish saint, it may be impossible to determine.[1] The name most probably represents a surviving tradition of some Druidical deity. This idea receives some support from the fact that, by the same people, "there were

[1] The researches of Drs Reeves and Skene have now established the identity of St Mourie. His name in Old Irish is Maelruba, later Maolrubha, corrupted into Mourie and Maree. He came from Ireland in 671, and in 673 he founded the Church of Applecross, from which "as centre he evangelised the whole of the western districts lying between Lochcarron and Lochbroom, as well as the south and west parts of the island of Skye, and planted churches in Easter Ross and elsewhere. The dedications to him show that his missionary work was very extensive" — (Skene). His grave at Applecross is called Cladh Maree, and it is from him that Loch Maree takes its name. — (Ed.).

"In 722, Saint Maelrubha (Applecross) is said to have been murdered by Norwegians at Urquhart (Ferintosh), in Ross. There was erected, says the Aberdeen Breviary, on the spot where he was slain a chapel of oak, which afterwards became the Parish Church of Urquhart. The church was afterwards a part of the prebend of the Treasurer of Ross." — (Origines Parochiales).

frequent approaches to some ruinous chapels, and circulating of them.'' The Presbytery also found ''that future events in reference specially to life and death, in taking of journeys, was expected to be manifested by a hole of a round stone, wherein they tried the entering of their head, which, if they would do it, to wit, be able to put in their heads, they expect their returning to that place; and, failing, they conceived it ominous.'' What effect would the application of this test and faith in this omen have on the hosts who travel in these restless days? If the old Highland proverb — ''A large head on a wise man, and a hen's head on a fool'' — be as true as it is trite, would not the reading of the omen require to be reversed in order to keep the most of them at home?

In Gairloch, during the same tour of visitation by the Presbytery, similar practices were found to prevail, as appears from the following minute, dated ''Kenlochewe, 9th Sept., 1656'': ''The Brethren, taking into their consideration the abominations within the parochin of Gairloch, in sacrificing of beests upon the 25 August, as also in pouring of milk upon hills as oblations, whose names are not particularlie signified as yet, referred to the diligence of the minister to mak search of thoas persounes and summoned them; and withal that by his private diligence he have searchers and tryers of everie corner of the cuntrey, especiallie about the Loch Mourie, of the most faithfulle and honest men he can find; and that such as are his elders he particularlie poseit concerning former practices, in what they know of thoas poore ones who are called Mourie his deviles, who receives the sacrifices and offerings on account of Mourie his poore ones, and that at least some of thoas be summoned to compeare before the Presbyterie until the rest be discovered.'' The Presbytery, at the same time, found ''that Mourie has his monuments and remembrances in several parochins within the Presbyterie, but more particularly in the parochins of Lochcarron, Lochalsh, Kintail, Containe, Foddertie, and Lochbroome.'' In spite of every effort to put them down, these ''heathenish practices'' continued to prevail for some time thereafter, for in 1678 the curate of Gairloch, Mr Roderick Mackenzie, summoned certain parties ''for sacrificing in ane heathenish manner in the island of St Ruffus, commonly called Eilean Mourie, in Lochewe, for recovering the health of Cirstane Mackenzie.'' What was then the state of that district, may help to give an idea of the gross darkness that must have overspread the whole Highlands a century before.

Of the ministers who then laboured in Ross-shire, not many names are remembered. The Gospel was fully and faithfully preached in some parishes in those days. In Tain and in Kincardine, in the Presbytery of Tain, there were godly ministers; in Kiltearn, and, for a short time, in Fodderty, in the Presbytery of Dingwall, and in Cromarty, in the Presbytery of Chanonry. It was in Kiltearn, under the ministry of Mr Hogg, that the most signal success attended the preaching of the Gospel; but there were movements elsewhere among the ''dry bones,'' and, throughout the county, souls were then gathered to Christ and to glory, as the first-fruits of Ross-shire unto God.

At the Restoration, not many of the ministers were found faithful in the day of trial. Mr M'Killigan, then minister of Fodderty, was the only one who at once demitted his charge. Mr Hogg of Kiltearn, Mr Anderson of Cromarty, and Mr Andrew Ross of Tain were deposed; and in 1665 Mr Thomas Ross of Kincardine resigned his living. All the other ministers clung to their stipends, and contrived to swallow piece-meal the ''black prelacy'' that was then thrust on the conscience of Scotland.

The conforming ministers were allowed to retain some relics of their former privileges, to reconcile them the more easily to their bondage. They, forsooth, held their meetings of Presbytery, and wrote minutes of their proceedings, which are still extant, and mixing the memories of other days with the dreams of the present, they might have cheated themselves into thinking that they were not Episcopalians after all. Their Bishops — for they had three in succession — humoured their dupes as other of their mitred brethren would not. They allowed them to meet in Presbytery, with a Moderator, Episcopally chosen, and an Archdeacon, who, in the Moderator's absence, might act as his substitute. When both these ''Bishops' brats'' were on a hunting expedition after some of ''the seditious ministers,'' or were required to wait on ''their Right

Reverend Father in Chanrie'' on the day appointed for the meeting
of Presbytery, ''the brethren'' were not allowed to transact any
business, and could only minute in their record that they had met
and done nothing. The only work allowed to them, at any time, was
to wade through all the vile details of the cases of discipline that
were reported to them, and then to pass them over to the Bishop for
decision; to examine candidates for orders, who were then required
to repair for ordination to the Bishop; and to report, for the
information of the Bishop and the Council, all they knew regarding
the ongoings of the outed ministers. They retained, from better
days, the practice of delivering, in rotation, ''an exercise and
addition'' on some passage of Scripture, at each meeting of their
so-called Presbytery; but, strict though they were in requiring an
apology for absence, the man who had ''to exercise'' was very often
''indisposed'' on the day of meeting.

In 1665 the Bishop sent an order to the Presbyteries ''requiring
them to use all diligence in celebrating the holy Sacrament of the
Supper.'' The men who, in former days, judged their congregations
''quite unfitted for such service,'' now, while their congregations
are in no better state than before, resolve to yield obedience to the
Bishop. In 1668 the Bishop ''ordains, by letter, that the brethren
preach on Christ's nativity day,'' and all the brethren afterwards
reported that they did so, except one, who was ''tender at the
time.''

In 1671 the effect of Episcopal drill becomes more apparent, and
they regulate their procedure most submissively, ''according to the
act passed by my Lord Bishop.'' In 1678 they would meet ''for
dispatching of Mr Roderick Mackenzie, Chanter, south, as Commissioner from the Synod of Ross to the Primate, in order to the
process delivered against Mr Hugh Anderson, late minister of
Cromartie''; and on the same year, ''the Moderator presented a
letter from the Right Reverend Father the Bishop, desiring that the
Moderator, with a select number of the brethren, should repair to
Chanrie to put a final period to Mr Hugh Anderson''; the Bishop
adding the words, ''his process,'' to his order, to meet the scruples
of the quondam Presbyterians. Thereafter, they continued to act

most zealously, as the Bishop's police, against the few faithful Christians who were left in the county, and who were troublers of the prelatic peace.

"The camel" given them to swallow in the test oath of 1681 caused a little higgling, which drew down upon them an imperious letter from the Bishop, whose threats were far more effectual than its logic. It had a sting in its tail which terrified the poor men, though the argument in the body of it must have failed to convince them; and so "all the brethren concluded to meet at Chanrie on Tuesday, the 28th December current, to close their resolution anent the test." Having bolted the oath, they lay down in their chains, and, excepting the intervals of disturbance caused by the conventicles at Kiltearn, Alness, and other places, they slept on till awakened by "the glorious revolution."

In 1690, Presbytery began to resume possession, but only very slowly could it do so. There were few ministers to whom places, occupied by them before the Restoration, were open. Mr Hogg returned to Kiltearn, but the labour of a few weeks sufficed to exhaust the remnant of strength which persecution had left in him; Mr Anderson resumed his work at Cromarty; and for a few months Mr M'Killigan laboured at Alness; but these, for nearly two years, were the only Presbyterian ministers who had been in the county. In 1693, though the ministers of Ross and of Sutherland were united in one Presbytery, there were only four out of the two counties whose names appear in the sederunt at any of their meetings; Mr Hugh Anderson, Cromarty, and Mr William Stewart, Kiltearn, being at that time the only Presbyterian ministers in Ross-shire, and Mr Walter Denune, Golspie, and Mr William Mackay, Dornoch, the only Presbyterian ministers in Sutherland.

A few of the Episcopal incumbents laid themselves open to deposition by their disloyalty, and some by their immorality, and the places of others were soon made vacant by death. But of these openings the Assembly could not take immediate advantage. The demand for ministers was beyond the supply. They had not learned to extemporise incumbents, as was the fashion in the days of the Tulchans, and of the more ambitious prelatists of later times.

Vacancies abounded, but they chose to wait till the breaches were repaired by the Lord, rather than to shovel in such rubbish as had filled them before.

The re-occupying of the county, even when supply was provided, was found to be more difficult than to take possession of it at first. Not only were the Episcopal incumbents on the field to employ all the influences which they had managed to acquire in opposition to the cause of the Gospel, but a strong political feeling was aroused, and directed by the Jacobite chieftains, alike against the reigning sovereign and against the Church which he had been the means of restoring. There were a few among the people who had hailed the Revolution with delight, and who, still more, rejoiced in the restoration of the Gospel to their land; but the number of such was small. In several parishes the first presentees had much opposition to encounter. In 1716, the minister of Gairloch was compelled to leave his parish, owing to the ill-treatment he received at the hands of both the laird and the people. His crops were destroyed, his home robbed, and he and his family were reduced to a state of starvation. In 1720, the presentee to Lochalsh was not allowed to preach at all in that parish, and for several years after he was first driven out of it, he could not venture to return to his charge. In 1717, the minister of Killearnan was refused by the heritors, who were bigoted Jacobites, any share of the maintenance due to him; his manse was razed to the ground; and, so incensed were the people against him under the instigation of the lairds, that his ministry was deserted, and his person in danger.

Even after the most of the charges in the Synod were supplied by Presbyterian ministers, the curates still hovered about them, and, by clandestine marriages and baptisms, and in various other ways, exerted a baneful influence on the feelings and habits of the people. In course of time these gad-flies were removed; and the only traces of "black prelacy" left in the county were a very few Episcopal chapels, the resorts of Jacobite lairds and their underlings, and of fugitives from Presbyterian discipline.

It was after the first quarter of the eighteenth century had passed that the best days of Ross-shire began. A few godly ministers were then scattered over the province of the Synod. In 1725, Mr James Fraser was ordained minister of Alness, and his labours were early and greatly blessed. Seven years thereafter Mr Porteous came to Kilmuir, and few ministers have been more successful than he. Mr Balfour of Nigg, Mr M'Phail of Resolis, Mr Beaton of Rosskeen, and Mr Wood of Rosemarkie, all famous men of God, were his contemporaries. Before the middle of the century the great revival of religion began, which spread its blessed influence alike over Highlands and Lowlands. At Nigg, Kilmuir, Rosskeen, and Rosemarkie, especially, the Lord's right hand wrought wonders of grace in "turning" many "from darkness to light"; but in other places throughout the county many souls were then gathered to the Lord. Under the ministry of such men as Fraser, Porteous, Beaton, Balfour, M'Phail, and Wood, the good work continued to advance and to spread, till the desert began indeed to "rejoice and blossom as the rose."

This extensive revival resulted from the blessing of the Lord on the stated preaching of the Gospel. It was preceded by much prayer. It began in the hearts and the closets of the people of the Lord. Its progress was attended by no unseemly excitement. There were no outcries or prostrations at public meetings in those days. It gave rise to no unwise multiplication of agents, means, and meetings. Deep impressions of their utter impotence under the power of sin, as well as of their utter inexcusableness under its guilt, with a distinct recognition of the necessity of regeneration and of the sovereignty of grace, distinguished the experience of the awakened. Attaining to a clear view of the foundation, object, and warrant of the "hope set before them" in the gospel, they grew up, under the skilful tuition of godly ministers, intelligent, exercised, and consistent Christians. An intense averseness to unsoundness, formality, and unwatchfulness distinguished them as a class. Few, very few, of those who were admitted into the confidence of the Church at that time ever belied their profession. They were, indeed, to Ross-shire, a preserving and seasoning salt, till the Lord removed them out of it.

In 1782,[1] there met at Kiltearn, on a communion occasion,

[1] "It was before 1792, if not in the above year. The year 1792 is called in

under the preaching of Dr Fraser of Kirkhill, perhaps as blessed a congregation as ever assembled in Scotland. Hundreds of God's people from the surrounding district were there, and all of them had as much of the comforting presence of the Lord as they were able to endure. It was then the culminating point of the spiritual prosperity of Ross-shire was reached. Under the ministry of the Calders, Macadam, Mackenzie, the Mackintoshes, Forbes, Macdonald, and others, the Lord's people continued to be edified, and souls were still ''added to the Church.'' But such days of power as were formerly enjoyed have never yet returned. Days of richer blessing shall verily yet be given; but ere they shall come the present generation may have passed, under the ''shame of barrenness,'' from the earth.

It is worthy of remark that it was at the climax of its spiritual prosperity the cruel work of eviction began to lay waste the hillsides and the plains of the north. Swayed by the example of the godly among them, and away from the influences by which less sequestered localities were corrupted, the body of the people in the Highlands became distinguished as the most peaceable and virtuous peasantry in Britain. It was just then that they began to be driven off by ungodly oppressors, to clear their native soil for strangers, red deer, and sheep. With few exceptions, the owners of the soil began

that district 'the year of the sheep' — 'bliadhna nan caorach.' The system of taking the hill grazing from the people and introducing sheep-farming then commenced. This roused the people; they assembled and resolved to drive all the sheep that had been introduced to the River Conon (there were no bridges on the rivers in those days) and let them sink or swim there. This roused the lairds in Ross- and Inverness-shires. The Sheriff-Depute of Ross-shire and the proprietors put their heads together. Sir Hector Munro of Novar, who was Colonel of the 42nd Regiment, summoned that regiment from Fort-George to Novar, where, it is said, there was music and dancing on the Sabbath. Some of those of the people who were engaged in the matter were laid hold of and brought before the Justiciary Court at Inverness, and were sentenced, but escaped from prison. Now it was on a Sabbath day about the early part of the autumn of 1792 the music and dancing was at Novar. I heard that the pious people in the country — and there were many at that time — noted the following, viz., that the gospel was as faithfully and purely preached in that part of Ross-shire after that date as it was before that date, but it was not followed with the same power as it had been before then.'' — (Dr Aird).

to act as if they were also owners of the people, and, disposed to regard them as the vilest part of their estate, they treated them without respect to the requirements of righteousness or to the dictates of mercy. Without the inducement of gain, in the very recklessness of cruelty, families by hundreds were driven across the sea, or were gathered, as the sweepings of the hillsides, into wretched hamlets on the shore. By wholesale evictions wastes were formed for the red deer, that the gentry of the nineteenth century might indulge in the sports of the savages of three centuries before. Of many happy households sheep walks were cleared for strangers, who, fattened amidst the ruined homes of the banished, corrupted by their example the few natives who remained. Meanwhile, their rulers, while deaf to the Highlanders' cry of oppression, were wasting their sinews and their blood on battle-fields, that, but for their prowess and their bravery, would have been the scene of their country's defeat.

CHAPTER II

THE MINISTERS OF ROSS-SHIRE

A LIST of all the ministers of Ross-shire would be a very checkered one. It would present many grades of talent, from the man of genius down to the dunce; many varieties of religion, from the man of singular godliness down to the scoffer; every variety of life, from the holy man of God down to the drunkard; and many shades of popularlity, from the man whom all revered down to the man whom all despised.

A roll of its ministers in its worst days would be much more uniform than such a roll at its best. There were times in Ross-shire when its ministers cared not to affect much godliness, and were not suspected of having any at all. Such, at least, were the two sets of curates, some of whom may have sunk further down in ignorance and immorality than the rest, but to eminence for learning and piety none of them were known to aspire. But in the best days of Ross-shire there was no monotony of character among the clergy. It was just then that strongly marked specimens of both the good and the bad might be found. The more eminent the Lord made his ministers, by the measure of grace which He gave them, the more difficult Satan must have found it to insert a seemly hypocrite among them. The places which were filled up by the enemy he succeeded in possessing, not by deceiving the judgment of the Church, but by employing the power of the world. The skilled labourers whom the Lord sent into His vineyard were not easily imitated, and the others would not try to be like them. Some of these, therefore, began to follow the lairds when they found they could not copy the preachers; they would be real gentlemen, and cared not about being real ministers at all. Others, too rude for the drawing-room, and too keen in their enmity to refrain from persecution, were given to annoying the ministers who preached, and the people who loved, the doctrines of grace. Some others were so gross in their conduct that they seemed as if Satan, despairing of fashioning them into plausible hypocrites, had let them fall into the mire to which their sensuality inclined them, that he might prepare them as a nuisance, since he could not use them as a snare. Getting them into the ministry, he had the power to keep them, on the elevation of their office, before the eyes of the faithful, that he might grieve their hearts by the vileness which could not possibly deceive them. Among the Lord's own ministers there was variety also. Some were more gifted, some more godly, and some more successful than others, but among them might surely be found men as like to their Master, and as fitted for their work, as Christ ever gave to the Church since the days of the Apostles.

The godly ministers of Ross-shire may be divided into three classes. There are a few whose names tower above those of all others, and to whom, by universal consent, the first place would be given. These alone are now to be specially noticed; but in the memories of those who are acquainted with the history of the Gospel in Ross-shire, about thirty names will rise up, forming a second class, of men who were faithful in their day and accepted in their work. But the list of these would not exhaust the whole number of the ministers whom the Lord claimed as His servants. Beneath them there wrought, with more slender gifts and with smaller success, some whose names are now scarcely remembered, but who were for Christ on the earth, and who are now with Him in heaven.

It was neither by talents, nor by learning, nor by oratory, nor was it by all these together that a leading place was attained by the ministers in the Highlands, but by a profound experience of the power of godliness, a clear view of the doctrines of grace, peculiar nearness to God, a holy life, and a blessed ministry. Without these, without all these, a high place would not be assigned to them either by the Lord or by men. Eminence thus reached is surely the holiest and the highest; and it is a healthful state of matters when the attainment of it otherwise is rendered impossible. In other portions of the Church a minister might become famous as an ecclesiastic, an orator, or a scholar, who, merely for his godliness, would be utterly unknown. But mere gifts and acquirements were but little accounted of in the north. Few opportunities for displaying them, apart from the pulpit, were presented to those who may have had them, and the unsanctified use of them there would earn only the distinction of disgrace. Most ungracious, indeed, would have been the treatment by the people of the north, in the good days of the Fathers, of such preaching as is to be found in "The Religion of Common Life," and even in "The Gospel in Ezekiel." Worthless, because Christ-less, would they have deemed the religion commended in the former; and even the latter, giving them rather more of the poetry in Guthrie than of the Gospel in Ezekiel, would have found but small favour at their hands.

But the ministry in Ross-shire furnishes no exception to the rule that, on the man whom He makes eminent in His Church, the Lord bestows excellent gifts, as surely as an unusual measure of grace. Among them were men of distinguished talent; a few of them were men of genius; and the lowest of them stood at least on a level with the average ministry of the Church in point of literary acquirements. If they earned no fame for mere talent and learning, it was because, having once cast their gifts and acquirements at the feet of their Master, they cared not to bear them aloft for the admiration of their fellows; and because they occupied places in a quiet portion of the Church from which they were not called to the construction or defence of the outworks — the service in which the lustre of talent and of learning finds most occasion to appear. They were allowed to devote themselves almost exclusively to the more spiritual duties of their calling; and they had learned, in that sphere, to dispense with "excellency of speech and of wisdom."

Each one of them would have been distinguished as a Christian, though he had never been a minister. There are ministers who find all their Christianity in their office, having had none of it before in their hearts. Far otherwise was it with the godly Fathers in Ross-shire. With two exceptions, they had all been Christians before they were office-bearers, and some of them from their earliest years. Nor were they ordinary Christians. Their deep experience of the work of the Spirit, their clear views of the doctrines of grace, their peculiar nearness to God, and their holy watchfulness, would have made them eminent among the godly, though they never had a place among the clergy. Each of them had his own peculiarity of experience, but all of them were deeply exercised in a life of godliness; each had his favourite department of truth, while lovingly embracing the whole, but all of them were "skilful in the word of righteousness"; some of them were favoured with more intimate communion with the Lord than the others, but they were all "a people near unto Him"; each one was distinguished by some peculiar grace, but they all lived "soberly, righteously, and godly in a present evil world." In every respect they differed from each other, but in their common resemblance to their Father in Heaven; but, owing to this, they were all recognised, even by the world, as brethren in the Lord.

As preachers, they were all remarkable. There are some who preach *before* their people, like actors on the stage, to display themselves and to please their audience. Not such were the *self-denied* preachers of Ross-shire. There are others who preach *over* their people. Studying for the highest, instead of doing so for the lowest, in intelligence, they elaborated learned treatises, which float like mist, when delivered, over the heads of their hearers. Not such were the *earnest* preachers of Ross-shire. There are some who preach *past* their people. Directing their praise or their censure to intangible abstractions, they never take aim at the views and the conduct of the individuals before them. They step carefully aside, lest their hearers should be struck by their shafts, and aim them at phantoms beyond them. Not such were the *faithful* preachers of Ross-shire. There are others who preach *at* their people, serving out in a sermon the gossip of the week, and seemingly possessed with the idea that the transgressor can be scolded out of the ways of iniquity. Not such were the *wise* preachers of Ross-shire. There are some who preach *towards* their people. They aim well, but they are weak. Their eye is along the arrow towards the hearts of their hearers, but their arm is too feeble for sending it on to the mark. Superficial in their experience and in their knowledge, they reach not the cases of God's people by their doctrine, and they strike with no vigour at the consciences of the ungodly. Not such were the *powerful* preachers of Ross-shire. There are others still, who preach *along* their congregation. Instead of standing with their bow in front of the ranks, these archers take them in line, and, reducing their mark to an individual, never change the direction of their aim. Not such were the *discriminating* preachers of Ross-shire. But there are a few who preach *to* the people directly and seasonably the mind of God in His Word, with authority, unction, wisdom, fervour, and love. Such as these last were the eminent preachers of Ross-shire.

They were all of the Lord's making, but each one was adapted to the place he had to fill, and to the work which was given him to do. While all of them were excellent, each of them was peculiar, and their variety was as necessary as their skill. In apt and striking illustration Porteous and Mackenzie excelled, and have left more memorable sayings behind them than any of the others; Calder and M'Phail preached in clear, unctuous words, filled full of Christ crucified, while from their manner and language all was carefully excluded that might withdraw the minds of their hearers from the spiritual import of the message which they carried; for exactness of exposition and precision of statement, Macadam and Forbes were second to none; Dr Mackintosh was eminent in solemnity and power; and for clearness and skill in unfolding the doctrines of grace, and in fervent appeals to the Christless, Fraser and Macdonald excelled them all.

Their preaching was remarkable for its completeness. It combined carefulness of exposition, fulness and exactness of doctrinal statement, a searching description of experimental godliness, and close application of truth to the conscience. The admixture of these elements, in wisely-adjusted proportions, constitutes the true excellence of preaching. Careful to ascertain the mind of God in His Word, they were not content merely to prefix a passage of Scripture as a motto to their sermon. They chose to preach from a text rather than to discourse on a subject. They did not try what they themselves could say about it, but to tell what the Lord said through it, to their hearers. But, while careful expounders, they were systematic theologians as well. They clearly saw, and they clearly taught, "the form of sound doctrine." No loose statement of doctrine would satisfy them, and yet no men were further than they from being frozen into the stiffness of a cold, lifeless orthodoxy. Their zeal for a sound creed was at least equalled by their desire for a godly experience and a holy life. They loved "the form of sound doctrine," but they also loved "the power of godliness." They insisted on a clear understanding of the former, but they also insisted on a deep experience of the latter. It is in fashion to speak of objective and subjective preaching, and to commend each by itself as excellent in its way; but surely that preaching is defective, that presents a statement of doctrine without any description of the experience which the application of that doctrine produces, or of the fruits in which that experience results; and preaching without distinct doctrinal statement is like attempting to build without a plummet or a plan. And their preaching was distinguished by the minuteness with which the Lord guided them to speak to the varied cases of their hearers. In this respect they were quite singular; and many marvellous instances of this might be given. Some of these might be easily accounted for. In dealing with the cases of God's people, a minister, acquainted with the power of godliness, will be sure to have a counterpart, in his own experience, of many of the fears, hopes, and enjoyments of those whom he addresses. Speaking from the heart, he will be sure to speak to the heart; declaring what he himself has felt, he will be sure to express the feelings of others. When the honour the Lord has been wont to put on the ordinance of preaching, and His tender care of His children are taken into account, who will limit the degree of minuteness to which the Lord's guidance may be given, in adapting the message sent by His servant to the varied feelings of the hearers? Words marvellously seasonable have been often thus spoken, to account for which no prophetic gift should be ascribed to the preacher. The pressing need of a beloved child had to be seasonably met, and the Lord revived, in the memory of His servant, a corresponding experience, and guided him to tell it, and this is often the whole secret of the matter. There have been, however, instances of "words in season" that cannot thus be explained. Some more direct guidance of the speaker's mind was required, and some more abrupt impression must have been produced of the case, to which the Lord was sending a leaf from the tree of life, or an arrow from the quiver of the law. Care will be taken that any such instances as may be given shall be accurately stated rather than satisfactorily explained.

Of all of them, without exception, it may be affirmed that they were scrupulously careful in their preparation for the pulpit. These were not men to offer to the Lord that which cost them nothing. Their aim in studying was not the construction of a finished or a pleasing sermon. Mere sermon-making was not their work. They sought to know what message the Lord was giving them, and to be prepared to deliver it in the manner most accordant with the gifts conferred on themselves, and most suitable to the circumstances and attainments of their hearers. Each had his own way of studying, as surely as his own way of preaching. Four of the Ross-shire Fathers were once comparing notes on this subject. "I like," one of them said, "to have my subject determined, and my skeleton arranged, on the Sabbath evening." "I devote," the second said, " "a portion of each day of the week to the preparation of my sermon." "I don't begin to write till Friday," the third said. "But I," added the fourth, "am so dependent on wind and tide, that I can act according to no rule; I sometimes have my sermon ready days before I deliver it, and sometimes it is not ready till it is preached." On another occasion the same number of eminent ministers united in declaring, as the result of their experience, that none had ever come to tell them of any part of what they had preached from memory having been felt to be "a word in season," and that any word, ascertained by them to have been fitly spoken, was suggested to their minds during the course of the sermon. This circumstance, so carefully removing all grounds of boasting, they, at the same time, regarded as not furnishing the shadow of a reason for relaxing their diligence in the careful preparation of their sermons.

All of them were distinguished as men of prayer. Without this, they would not have had their godliness as Christians, nor their success as ministers. One of them would spend whole nights in prayer; another would forget his daily meals amidst the wrestlings of the closet; and in the study of another the rug on which he usually knelt would, in a few months, be quite worn through. But all of them, like these, were given unto prayer, and were admitted into peculiar nearness to the Lord. Their abounding in prayer made it safe and healthful to abound also in labours. Their public work was to them no wasting bustle, for in communion with the Lord their strength was recruited in the closet. Wrestling for grace with the Lord, and labouring with grace for the Lord, no blight was permitted to rest on their soul or their service. Prevailing with God as they pled for men, they prevailed with men as they pled for God.

As pastors, they watched for souls as those who must give an account unto God. Commanding the respect of the people, they were allowed to deal with them according to the authority of their office. They were strict and faithful, but tender and wise in the exercise of discipline. They were not much given to the formalities of stated visiting. It was not their habit to cross a certain number of thresholds every year. They did what was better for themselves and their flocks, for they visited them often in spirit, as they went to carry them on their hearts to the footstool of mercy. They obtained a more thorough knowledge of the views and feelings of their people, from one course of catechising, than they could from the perfunctory visiting of a lifetime; and if there was awanting to them, from the people, the merely carnal attachment that may be won by the civilities of ''the minister's call,'' the authority of their office was intact; and even from the conscience of the unconverted their godly life failed not to secure its tribute of respect.

The name of Thomas Hogg is the earliest that rises into eminence. From the interesting memoir of him which has been so widely circulated, it is evident that, while both a gentleman and a scholar, he was a Christian of singular godliness, enjoying very intimate communion with God, and a minister of rare devotedness, whose labours were abundantly blessed.[1]

Next in eminence, among those of the five non-conforming ministers of Ross-shire, stands the name of John M'Killigan.[2] He received a unanimous call from the people of Fodderty, September 4, 1655. On the 25th of the same month, he writes to the Presbytery, "that divers difficulties and perplexities made him unable to give a peremptory answer for the time." He was then in Morayshire, and thither Mr Hogg was twice sent by the Presbytery to deal with him in reference to the call. In the month of January following, he intimated his acceptance to the Presbytery, and his ordination took place on the 26th of February, 1656. Of his ministry at Fodderty no account can be given. In 1661 he unhesitatingly and at once took his stand against Prelacy. He was then the only minister who did so; for Mr Hogg was unable, owing to the state of his health, to bear any public testimony so soon, and the others remained for some time in their charges. A presentation was offered to him by the patron, but as "he reckoned the acceptance of that as destroying the foundation which God had laid in His Church, to the maintenance of which he was bound by solemn oath," he conclusively declined to accept it. In 1663 he was summarily ejected from his manse, which he continued to occupy after demitting his charge, to make room for Mr John Mackenzie, who, swollen by Prelacy into the vastness of an archdeacon, required the whole house to contain him. In the same year he is summoned

[1] In the old records of the Presbytery of Dingwall there is a full account of the "Trials" of Thomas Hogg. On the 17th October, 1654, the members of Presbytery and the congregations met in the church of Kiltearn to hear Hogg's "trial" sermon. He was then in the 27th year of his age. The text was Matt. ix. 6. When the sermon was preached the people were asked if they had anything against Mr Hogg being ordained as their pastor. They unanimously replied, No. On the 24th October, 1654, Mr Hogg was admitted to the pastorate.

[2] John M'Killigan, according to tradition, was born in the parish of Cawdor about 1630. He was licensed by the Presbytery of Forres, 28th March, 1655. Frequent notices of him appear in "Brodie's Diaries." He married Catherine Munro, daughter of the laird of Culcraggie, parish of Alness, who had as her dowry the small estate of Balchraggan, in the same parish. It was here Mr M'Killigan took up his abode after his ejection from Fodderty, and preached in a chapel erected on his property.

to give his reasons to the conclave of curates, his former co-Presbyters, for not asking from any of them baptism for his child; and, having been cited by the Bishop before his diocesan meeting, and refusing to appear, a sentence of deposition was passed against him, "for his absenting himself from the diocesan meeting, his not answering the citation to appear before him when called, and his preaching, praying, and reasoning against prelatical government."

Removed from Fodderty, he took up his residence on his own property at Alness. Till 1676 he continued to preach there and in other places to the few who would assemble to hear him, and his labours were greatly blessed by the Lord. A strong desire having been felt, by those who profited by his preaching, to partake of the Sacrament of the Supper, though under the ban of the Council and the watchful eyes of Bishop Paterson's police, he resolved to dispense that ordinance in September, 1675. The little congregation met in the house of the Dowager Lady of Fowlis at Obsdale, in the parish of Rosskeen. Mr M'Killigan was assisted by Mr Hugh Anderson,[1] minister of Cromarty, and Mr Alexander Fraser, minister of Deviot.[2] Mr Anderson preached the preparation sermon on Saturday, Mr M'Killigan officiated on Sabbath in the forenoon, and Mr Fraser in the afternoon, and Mr M'Killigan preached the thanksgiving discourse on Monday. During this last service, there

[1]Hugh Anderson of Cromarty was promoted from being Regent in the University and King's College, Aberdeen; installed in 1656; deprived by the Acts of Parliament in 1662, but was allowed to remain some years, probably till after engaging in the communion service at Obsdale, when he retired to his own property of Udol. By the Act of Parliament, 1690, he was restored. He was a member of Assembly in 1692, and the senior minister on the roll when the Presbytery of Ross was constituted, 25th April, 1693. He died on the 3rd of June, 1704, aged 74. (Scott's Fasti).

[2] Alexander Fraser was descended from the family of Fruid, in Tweeddale, and was brother of Robert Fraser, advocate, Edinburgh. He was translated from Abbotshall to Deviot, and admitted there on the 31st August, 1664. He was deposed in 1672 for espousing the persecuted cause. He afterwards became chaplain in the family of Ludovick Grant of Freughie, who, for allowing him to preach there, not preventing the attendance of his wife on such occasions, and withdrawing himself from ordinances, was fined £295. Mr Fraser survived the Revolution, and returned to Abbotshall. (Scott's Fasti).

was such a plentiful effusion of the Spirit, that the oldest Christians then present declared they had never enjoyed such a time of refreshing before. "In short," says Wodrow, "there were so sensible and glorious discoveries made by the Son of Man, and such evident presence of the Master of Assemblies, this day and the preceding, the people seemed to be in a transport, and their souls filled with heaven, and breathing thither while they were upon the earth; and some were almost at that 'Whether in the body or out of the body, I cannot tell.'" A man, hitherto careless about the state of his soul, had gone to that blessed meeting, impelled by mere curiosity, like the chief publican of old. The God of Zaccheus met him at Obsdale; and on his return from the meeting, one of his neighbours said to him, "What a fool you were to have gone; you will suffer the loss of all your goods for what you have done." "You are more to be pitied," he replied, "for not having been there; as for me, if the Lord would maintain in me what I hope I have won to, I would not only part with my cow and my horse, and these are my only earthly possessions, but with my head likewise if called to it."

Information having been given to the Bishop, by some of his spies, of Mr M'Killigan's intention to dispense the sacrament, he instigated Sir Roderick Mackenzie of Findon to send a party of soldiers to apprehend him. On Sabbath, while the little congregation was assembled at Obsdale, the soldiers came to Alness, expecting that Mr M'Killigan would have dispensed the sacrament there. To make amends for their disappointment, they began to pillage the minister's orchard, and, finding his apples to be particularly good, they remained long enough in the garden to allow them to close the forenoon service at Obsdale. The soldiers then received information of the actual meeting place, but, before they could reach it, the congregation had dispersed, and Mr M'Killigan was safe in his hiding-place. Missing him, the party sent to apprehend him returned; and, after they were gone, the ministers and people assembled again, and found that the Bridegroom had reserved the best wine to the close. But in the strength of the food then provided, the Christians who feasted at Obsdale had to go many days. Mr

M'Killigan was compelled to abscond, and for several years he and his flock were prevented from meeting together again.

Having gone to Cromarty to baptise the child of Mr Anderson, the deposed Presbyterian minister there, he was apprehended by a party of the Earl of Seaforth's followers. The night before his apprehension "he was trysted," says Wodrow, "with an odd enough passage, which he could not but remark. When he fell asleep he dreamed that there were three men come to the house to apprehend him. He was no observer of dreams, and, therefore, when he awakened he endeavoured to be freed of the thoughts of what he had been dreaming, and composed himself to sleep; but, upon his falling asleep, he dreamed it a second time, and awoke; and, again, after he had essayed to banish the thoughts of it, and falling asleep again, he dreamed it a third time. This awakened him with some concern, and he began to apprehend there might be more than ordinary in it, and fell under the impression that bonds and imprisonment were abiding him, and arose to compose himself, by committing his case to the Lord." Before he was dressed, the party sent to apprehend him were in the house. Confined for some time in the prison at Fortrose, he was afterwards removed to Nairn. Kindness shown to him by Sir Hugh Campbell of Cawdor provoked his accusers to insist on his removal to Edinburgh. After lying in the Tolbooth for a short time, he was sent as a prisoner to the Bass. The time spent by him there, which his enemies desired to make a season of distress, the Lord so sweetened by His presence that he could say — "Since I was a prisoner, I dwelt at ease and securely." But while his soul was joyful in the Lord, his body contracted the disease which ultimately terminated in his death. In 1679, he was liberated on bail, offered by Sir Hugh Campbell, who had formerly befriended him. Returning to Ross-shire, he resumed his work among the little flock that gathered around him in Alness, much to the joy of his people, and as much to the annoyance of the curates. But in 1683 he was again apprehended, and sent to the Bass. It was again to him a Bethel. Becoming dangerously ill, he petitioned for liberty to remove to Edinburgh, and the Council, on the intercession of Sir Hugh Campbell, granted his request. His health not improving, he was permitted, in 1686, to return to Ross-shire, where he continued to officiate in a meeting-house, erected by his attached followers in Alness, till the Revolution. Called in 1688 to Inverness, his people, owing to the state of his health, consented to his removal, but he preached there but seldom. Exhausted by all his labours and sufferings, his bodily strength rapidly declined, and he entered into his rest on the 8th of June, 1689.

In 1725, Mr James Fraser [1] was ordained minister of Alness. He was presented by the Presbytery, and was at first acceptable to all the people; but some of the lairds organised a factious opposition to his induction, using all their influence with their retainers and tenants against him. The Session and all the communicants remained steadfast, in the face of all the power of the lairds, but a great number of the people who had at first signed his call were induced to oppose him as the time for ordaining him approached. When the Presbytery met to induct him, they found the doors of the church shut and guarded against them, and the solemn service was conducted in a corner of the graveyard. An appeal against the ordination was taken to the Synod, and thereafter to the Assembly, but the Presbytery's conduct was ultimately approved of, and Mr Fraser confirmed in his charge. His induction did take place in the face of opposition, but the Presbytery were, in this case, in conflict only with those who interfered with the free choice of the people.

[1] James Fraser was ordained by the Presbytery of Chanonry, 6th November, 1723; ordained at Alness, 17th February, 1726; and entered into his rest, 5th October, 1769, in the 69th year of his age, and the 44th of his ministry. His father, John Fraser, who was minister of Alness from 1696 to 1711, suffered severely in the persecution. He went to New England, and about 1686 married Jean Moffat from Tweeddale, then a refugee from persecution like himself. He was translated from Glencross; he was laird of Pitcalzian, in the parish of Nigg; and his second son, James, was born in 1700. Between the father, John, and James, his son, Daniel M'Kiligan, son of John M'Kiligan, the Covenanter, was minister of Alness, having been translated from Kilmuir-Easter in 1714. He departed in the summer of 1723. James Fraser was a man of singular wisdom and great integrity, and steady friendship. He was a faithful counsellor; while his courteous behaviour as a gentleman, his piety as a Christian, and his great learning and knowledge as a divine, made him highly acceptable to all ranks. His notable work, ''The Scripture Doctrine of Sanctification,'' was published in Edinburgh in 1774. (Scott's Fasti).

Mr Fraser is the only one of all the Ross-shire Fathers who is well known as an author. His work on sanctification gives the most satisfactory explanation of that difficult portion of Scripture expounded in it, which has yet been produced. For exact analysis, polemical skill, and wise practical application of the truth, there are very few works which excel it. The specimens of his sermons which have been published entitle him to a very high place among the true preachers of the Gospel. Full, clear, and unctuous in their statements of Gospel truth, close and searching in their practical uses of doctrine, tender and wise in the counsels and encouragements given to believers, and solemn and powerful in appeals to the unconverted, they furnish a strong contrast to the fashionable preaching of these days, with its vague, hazy statements of doctrine, its wholesale application of Gospel comforts, and its flowers to please the taste, instead of arrows to pierce the conscience of the ungodly.

His preaching, at least during a great part of his ministry, was mainly directed to the awakening and conversion of sinners, and was not so edifying and consoling to the Lord's people as that of some others of the Fathers in Ross-shire. He did preach Christ crucified, and spake comfort to the broken-hearted, but this was not the peculiarity of his preaching. But the preponderance of the other element was of God, and He greatly blessed his preaching for fulfilling the end to which it was mainly directed. Many were awakened under his ministry, but some of these went elsewhere to get healing for their wounds. Each Sabbath not a few of his people were accustomed to go to Kilmuir to hear the famous Mr Porteous. So many were at last in the habit of going, that the Kilmuir congregation began to complain of the overcrowded state of the church; and though willing to bear some inconvenience for the sake of those who could not find the Gospel at home, they had no patience for the fugitives from Alness. His Session at last spoke to Mr Porteous about it, and begged of him to confer with Mr Fraser, ''for the people who come from Alness,'' they said, ''tell us that their minister preaches, almost so exclusively, the law, that those who seek the bread of life must starve under his ministry, and are compelled to come hither for food and for healing.'' Meeting Mr

Fraser soon after that, at a funeral, Mr Porteous said to him, "It gives me, my dear brother, grief of heart to see some of your people in the church of Kilmuir every Sabbath. My elders tell me that those who come to us complain of your preaching almost entirely to the unconverted, and that the 'poor in spirit' can get no food for their souls. Now, my dear brother, if the Lord gives it to you, I pray you not to withhold their portion from the people of the Lord, which you can dispense to them as I never could." "My dear brother," was Mr Fraser's striking reply, "when my Master sent me forth to my work, He gave me a quiver full of arrows, and He ordered me to cast these arrows at the hearts of His enemies till the quiver was empty. I have been endeavouring to do so, but the quiver is not empty yet. When the Lord sent you forth, He gave you a cruse of oil, and His orders to you were to pour the oil on the wounds of broken hearted sinners till the cruse was empty. Your cruse is no more empty than is my quiver. Let us both then continue to act on our respective orders, and as the blessing from on high shall rest on our labours, I will be sending my hearers with wounded hearts to Kilmuir, and you will be sending them back to Alness rejoicing in the Lord." Quite overcome with this beautiful reply, Mr Porteous said, "Be it so, my beloved brother"; and, after a warmer embrace than they had ever exchanged before, they parted. Surely this was a rare exhibition of self-denial and brotherly love!

A cold, unfeeling, bold, unheeding wordly woman was his wife. Never did her godly husband sit down to a comfortable meal in his own house, and often would he have fainted for sheer want of needful sustenance but for the considerate kindness of some of his parishioners. She was too insensate to try to hide her treatment of him, and well was it for him, on one account, that she was. His friends thus knew of his ill-treatment, and were moved to do what they could for his comfort. A godly acquaintance arranged with him to leave a supply of food in a certain place beside his usual walk, of which he might avail himself when starved at home. Even light and fire in his study were denied to him on the long, cold winter evenings, and as his study was his only place of refuge from the cruel scourge of his wife's tongue and temper, there, shivering and in the dark, he used to spend his winter evenings at home. Compelled to walk in order to keep himself warm, and accustomed to do so when preparing for the pulpit, he always kept his hands before him as feelers in the dark, to warn him of his approaching the wall at either side of the room. In this way he actually wore a hole through the plaster at each end of his accustomed beat, on which some eyes have looked that glistened with light from other fire than that of love at the remembrance of his cruel wife. But the godly husband had learned to thank the Lord for the discipline of this trial. Being once at a Presbytery dinner alone, amidst a group of moderates, one of them proposed, as a toast, the health of their wives, and, turning to Mr Fraser, said, as he winked at his companions, "You, of course, will cordially join in drinking to this toast." "So I will and so I ought," Mr Fraser said, "for mine has been a better wife to me than any one of yours has been to you." "How so?" they all exclaimed. "She has sent me," was the reply, "seven times a day to my knees when I would not otherwise have gone, and that is more than any of you can say of yours." On the day on which her godly husband entered into his eternal rest, and a very few hours after his death, some of the elders, on learning the sad tidings, hurried with stricken hearts and in tears to the manse. To their horror, they found Mrs Fraser outside feeding her poultry. Approaching her, one of them said, sobbing as he spoke, "So Mr Fraser has gone to his rest." "Oh, yes; the poor man died this morning," she said, as she scattered the corn among the fowls; "if you want to see the body, you may go in — chick, chick, chick." Whether horror of the living or sorrow for the dead was the deepest feeling in the good men's breasts, both must have mingled in the anguish of their hearts as they hurried to the chamber of the dead.

Seven years after Mr Fraser's induction at Alness, Mr John Porteous[1] was ordained minister of Kilmuir. He was born in

[1] John Porteous' grandfather came to Inverness with the army of Cromwell, and settled there, where his grandson was born. Had his degree from the University and King's College, Aberdeen, 29th March, 1720; licensed by the Presbytery of Elgin, 24th October, 1727; called, August 8th, and ordained 27th November, 1734. In 1745, George, Earl of Cromarty, prepared to join

Inverness. In his youth he received an excellent education, and became distinguished as a classical scholar. Soon after his licence, he was presented to Daviot, but the people of that parish would not receive him, and he was not one who would consent to be intruded into a charge. The people may err, as well as patrons, as did the people of Daviot on this occasion; but when the former err, it is in the abuse of a power which rightfully belongs to them, but when the latter presents an unsuitable minister, he doubly sins, for he has usurped a power that belongs to others, and employs it to the injury of those from whom he has robbed it. At Kilmuir he was cordially received by the body of the people. At the very outset of his ministry, he got his place as a man of God over his flock, and the blessing of the Lord rested on his earliest labours among them. As a preacher, he was quite peculiar. Of all the famous preachers in the north, next to "Mr Lachlan," he was the most successful in riveting the attention of his hearers. His power of illustration was great, and he could make a safe and dexterous use of allegory. His metaphors were always apt, if not always poetical. His care was to use them as illustrations rather than as ornaments. He never tried to embellish, but he laboured to simplify his discourses.

In his pastoral intercourse with his people, he was remarkably

the Pretender; on this his pastor called for him, and earnestly and affectionately remonstrated with him against such a course, which so irritated the noble peer that he ordered Mr Porteous to leave the castle. At his exit he declared, "It won't be long until the grass will be growing in the room out of which you have ordered me," which was literally fulfilled before Mr Porteous died, 17th January, 1775. "He was pre-eminently popular; his distinguishing characteristics were sublimity and spirituality of doctrine, patriarchal simplicity of diction and manner; a deep insight into the human constitution, the power of embodying his thoughts in forcible language, and thus carrying demonstration to the conscience. He possessed a brilliant imagination, which was so thoroughly imbued with Christian truth that it always ministered instruction, and enabled him to enlighten and edify his hearers." The Rev. William Porteous, minister of Rafford, was a brother. He was schoolmaster of Forres; licensed by the Presbytery, 13th June, 1727; called, October 12th, and ordained, 28th December, same year; departed, 3rd January, 1738, in the 11th year of his ministry. He married Helen M'Intosh, who died 30th March, 1798, and had a daughter, Jean, who married the Rev. William M'Kenzie of Tongue. The brothers, John and William Porteous, were relatives of Beilby, afterwards Bishop of London. — *Fasti Eccl. Scoti.*

winning and wise. Being fond of flowers, and afraid that he might forget his flock while engaged in cultivating his garden, he connected with each plant he reared the name of some godly parishioner or acquaintance. It was, to his mind, congenial employment to trace analogies between the varieties of flowers in his garden, and the varieties of character in his parish; and having succeeded in attaching each flower to its antitype, in his mind and memory, his employment in the garden never allowed him to forget that he was a watchman for souls. A broken-hearted, humble, timid Christian once found the minister in his garden when he called upon him. Bringing him beside a plant of violet, and pointing to it, "There you are," Mr Porteous said. "That dark uncomely thing, without flower or fruit, is truly like me," remarked his visitor, as he looked down on it. "Yes, it is indeed like you," rejoined the minister, as he opened up its leaves and exposed its flowers, "for it is a lowly fragrant plant, that usually hides its beauty, and whose sweetness is most felt, when it is most closely searched and pressed." A young man, who had been recently awakened, came to him as he was walking among his flowers. He described his feelings, and the minister listened in silence, but he had no flower to which to point the inquirer, and did not speak a word to him, till a toad was observed crawling across the path, on which they were walking. "Do you see that?" the minister asked, pointing to the toad. "I do," the young man answered, and they passed on, and, without another word from the minister, they parted. A second and a third time, there was a repetition of what occurred at the first interview. But when, a fourth time, the youth's attention was called to the crawling toad, "It would be well for me," he said, "were I that toad without a soul that can be lost for ever." "I can speak to you now," his minister said. He judged his wound not to have been deep enough before, but now he entered into close and earnest conversation with him about the way of healing. There may have been thereafter a type of this young man among the flowers in the minister's garden.

Enjoying much of the Lord's presence in preaching, and a rich blessing resting on his labours, it was no wonder that he should have to bear many a rude assault of "the wicked one." He could be no stranger to Satan's devices; for having so many of the Lord's children to feed, it was needful that he should, as their pastor, be passed through their trials, besides, as a Christian, experiencing his own. Speaking to a pious woman once of some temptation by which he was greatly afflicted, she said, "Be patient under the Lord's training; the temptations of his people must be given seven-fold to the minister, if he is to be a minister indeed."

His personal appearance was striking. Unusually tall, erect in his figure, light in his step, and scrupulously exact in his dress, he was very unlike the picture a Southron would be disposed to draw of the Highland country minister of a century ago. He never married, and, unburdened with the cares of this life, it might truly of him have been said: "He careth for the things that belong to the Lord, how he may please the Lord." He quietly fell asleep in Jesus, in the attitude of prayer, alone with the Lord, on the seventh day of January, 1775, in the eighty-fourth year of his age. His ministry in Kilmuir extended over forty-three years.

The following notes of Mr Porteous' preaching were often given, with great effect, in Gaelic, by Dr Macdonald. The reader must find out for himself the lessons of the allegories. It is impossible to translate them without blunting their point; but even in starched English they may give an idea of how Mr Porteous succeeded in arresting the attention of his hearers, in getting access to their understanding, and in fixing the truth in their memory:

"A traveller, while passing through a desert, was overtaken by a storm. So violent was the tempest, that he at last despaired of surviving it. Just as hope died within him, his eye was caught by a light that glimmered in the distance, and he hastened his steps to reach it. Arriving at the place where it shone, he sees an open house, entering which, he finds himself in an apartment, with a fire on the hearth, and a seat placed beside it. He sat down, and, making himself as comfortable as possible, he felt happy at his escape from the storm, that was still raging without. On entering, he had seen nothing but what has already been noticed; but about midnight, happening to look round, he saw a dead body lying in the corner of the room. The corpse having begun to rise, as he looked at it, the poor man became dreadfully frightened, and as the dead was rising higher and higher, he rushed to the door to escape from the house. But the storm was still so violent that he dared not go out, and no choice was left to him but to return to his place by the fire. For a time the corpse was at rest, but he could not keep his eyes off the corner where it lay; and as he looked, it began to rise, and now higher than before. Again he sprung from his seat, but, instead of rushing to the door, he this time fell on his knees. As he knelt, the dead body lay back again, and he ventured once more to his seat by the hearth. He had not long been there when up again rises the corpse, and now still higher than formerly; so on his knees again he fell. Observing that only while he was kneeling the dead body lay still, he rose not again from his knees till the day had broken, and the shadows fled away.''

''A farmer in Kilmuir was once engaged in thrashing corn. Having been busy all day, there was a considerable heap on the floor at night as the result of his labour. But when he came back to his barn next morning all the thrashed corn was away. This occurred a second and a third time, till the farmer could bear it no longer. So he resolved to watch all night, as well as work all day. Having done so, he had not been long waiting when the thief appeared, and began to gather up the corn. Leaping upon him, the farmer tried to put him down, that he might either bind him, or hold him there till help arrived. But the thief proved the stronger of the two, and he had laid the farmer on his back, and had almost quite strangled him, when a friend came to his rescue. Having hold of the thief, after the farmer was on his legs again, his friend said to him, 'What will be done to the thief?' 'Oh, bind him,' was the answer, 'and give him to me on my back, and I will set off at once with him to the prison at Tain.' His friend did as he requested, and off set the farmer with his burden. But as he went out of sight of his friend, in a hollow of the road, the thief, with one effort, breaking the cords that bound him, fell upon the farmer, and gave him even a rougher handling than before. He would utterly have perished had not his faithful friend just come up in time again to save him. 'What will now be done?' his friend again asked. The answer was the same as before, only he added, 'I will be more careful this time.' So again he started with his troublesome burden on his back, and all was quiet, till he came to a dark part of the road, through the woods of Calrossie, when the fastenings were again broken, and the farmer maltreated even worse than before. Once again his friend comes to his help, but now the farmer would not part with him till he accompanied him to the prison. His request was granted, the jail reached, the thief locked up, and the farmer, forgetting his friend in his delight at getting rid of his tormentor, with a light step, set out for his home. Just as he had banished all fear from his heart, and was indulging in anticipations of peace for the future, in a moment the thief, having escaped from his cell and hurried to overtake him, sprang upon him from behind, and, with even more than his former fury, threw the poor farmer to the ground, and would have now killed him outright had not the wonted help just come 'in the time of need.' Once again his friend asked, 'What will now be done?' The farmer, worried and wearied, cast himself at his feet, and seizing him with both hands, cried, 'Let the day never dawn on which thou and I shall for a moment be parted, for without thee I can do nothing.' ''

''The eagle is said to renew its age. Old age comes on, and its end seems near, but, instead of passing out of life, it passes into youth again. It is commonly believed in the Highlands that its decay is owing to its bill becoming so long and so bent that it cannot take up its food, and that on that account, it pines from want of nourishment. The manner in which it is said to renew its age is by letting itself fall on a rock, by which means its bill is broken down to its proper size, its power to feed is restored, and youth begins again. That is but a legend, but this is truth, even that thy soul's strength, O believer, can only be renewed by thy letting thyself fall on Christ, the rock of ages.''

Mr Hector M'Phail,[1] of Resolis, was a minister for several years

---

[1] Mr Hector M'Phail was a native of Inverness; was licensed by the Presbytery of Inverness, 20th December, 1746, and ordained 22nd September, 1748; departed, 23rd January, 1774, in the 58th year of his age, and the 26th of his ministry. A man of singular worth, and unaffected piety, whose manner in

before his conversion. He had married a daughter of the godly Mr Balfour, minister of Nigg. She had been one of Mr Porteous' hearers, and had profited greatly by his preaching. Feeling painfully the difference between her husband's doctrine and that to which she had been accustomed, she told him, on a Sabbath morning soon after their marriage, that her soul was starving, and that, as all must give place to her care for its welfare, she had resolved to go on that day across to Kilmuir. He offered no opposition; he even accompanied her to the ferry. It was a sad journey the pious wife took that day to Kilmuir. Arriving at the manse before the hour for beginning the service in church, Mr Porteous was not a little surprised to see her, and, on meeting her, asked very anxiously why she had come. She told him that, as her soul was famished at Resolis, she was compelled to come for the bread of life to the place where she had been wont to receive it. Mr Porteous retired to his study, and, on rejoining her, said, "If I am not greatly deceived, you will not long have the same reason for leaving Resolis, for I expect that the Lord will soon give you, by the hand of your husband, the very finest of the wheat." His expectation was not disappointed. After parting with his wife on that morning, the fact

meeting any individual was to press on his consideration the ministry of reconciliation; in this he had a happy talent, and the solemn and affectionate exhortations which he offered not unfrequently left a deep impression. On visiting at one time Mr Calder, minister of Croy, he found him greatly distressed that a respectable farmer in the neighbouring part of Petty, whose wife had become violently insane, had determined to consult the Roman Catholic clergyman at Strathglass, in the expectation he could remove her disease. Both ministers waited on the farmer, and attempted to persuade him against what he desired. Failing in this, they went to the farm-house to offer such consolations as were in their power, and it led to a request that Mr M'Phail should offer up prayer in behalf of the sufferer, which was done with even more than usual fervour and earnestness, in which he used the following language: — "O Thou who are three times holy, I implore Thee not to allow me to rise from my knees, should they rot to the earth, until Thou makest it visibly known here that there is a God in Israel." The prayer was speedily heard and answered, as before the pious and good man rose from his prostration the patient was loosened from her bonds, and so calmed and restored that she sat up and conversed with him and the others in a sound mind, giving glory to God. Mr M'Phail had two sons in the ministry, James, of Daviot, and William, of the Scottish Church, Rotterdam. — *Fasti Eccl. Scoti.*

of her desertion of his ministry made a deep impression on Mr M'Phail's mind. Conscience testified that she was right: a deep sense of his unfitness for the work of the ministry was produced, and a process of conviction then began, that extended over several years. At last, he resolved to demit his charge, and to declare his resolution of doing so publicly before his congregation. With this view, he sent for Mr Fraser, Alness, to preach on a weekday in his church, and to intimate, after sermon, his resignation of his charge. Mr Fraser came and preached, but with no intention of giving the required intimation. During the sermon delivered on that day, Mr M'Phail's bonds were loosed, and before the service was over, he was in no mood to turn his back on the work of preaching Christ to sinners. Full of hope and gladness, he escorted Mr Fraser next day to the Alness ferry, and on his way back, he called at the house of one of his elders, who had spent many an hour wrestling with the Lord for his minister. ''What news to-day, Mr M'Phail?'' the elder asked. ''Good news,'' he said; ''Hector M'Phail is not to preach to you any more.'' ''Oh, I expected other news than that,'' the elder said, ''for I don't reckon that to be good news.'' ''Hector M'Phail is not to preach any more,'' his minister explained, ''but the Spirit of the Lord is to preach to you through him.'' ''Oh, that is good news, indeed,'' cried the elder in an ecstacy of joy. From that day till his death, Mr M'Phail was one of the most faithful, fervent, prayerful, and successful of ministers.

Remembering his unfaithfulness during the years of his ignorance, he had resolved never to omit an opportunity of speaking to a fellow-creature about the things belonging to his peace. He was enabled to fulfil his vow. The cases of Luke Heywood and the Highland kitchen-maid are well-known instances of how the Lord countenanced his faithful dealing with individuals.

He was much given to pastoral visitation of his parish. Throwing the rein on the neck of the well-known grey pony, as he mounted after breakfast, at whatever door it stopped he alighted and entered the house. The neighbours would immediately assemble, and he would expound a portion of Scripture and pray with them. Then, remounting, he would go, as the pony carried him, to some other place, and would occupy the remainder of the day in the manner in which he began it. On one of his excursions through the parish, he was observed striking with his cane a dog that lay beside the door of a house as he passed. Being asked why he had done so, he answered, ''He was so like myself, as he lay dumb and sleeping at his post, that I could not hold my cane off his back.''

Seated on one occasion, at dinner, in the house of one of his parishioners, along with some of his elders, he rose suddenly from the table, and, going out of the house, was seen by those whom he left behind walking hurriedly towards a wood not far from the house. There was a small lake in the wood, on the margin of which he found a woman just about to cast herself into the water. She had come from the parish of Alness, and, distracted and despairing, was driven by the Tempter to suicide. Mr M'Phail arrived just in time to intercept her from her purpose, and, preaching Christ to her disconsolate soul as ''able to save to the uttermost,'' this poor sinner was then and there disposed and enabled to ''flee for refuge to the hope set before'' her. Her after-life amply proved the genuineness of her conversion. But Satan will have his revenge. He suggested to Mr M'Phail that this woman was sent by him to Resolis because the shepherds across the water were too wakeful to allow him an opportunity of accomplishing his purpose in their parishes. When Mr Fraser heard of it, he said, ''That poor sinner was sent to Resolis because I was unfit for dealing with her case.''

As a preacher, he was peculiarly edifying to the people of the Lord. He could deal with their cases more closely and more tenderly than almost any other minister in his day. He does not appear to have been so careful in the composition of his sermons as some others of the fathers in Ross-shire. He was careful to feel, rather than to arrange, the doctrine which he preached, but what his discourses wanted of order was well made up by their unction and freshness. Having to preach on a Sabbath in Petty, and after a large congregation had assembled to hear him, he was in the wood, without sermon or text, wrestling with the Lord. The hour for beginning the service had long passed before Mr M'Phail was seen approaching the tent; but of all the remarkable sermons he ever preached, the one he preached that day was perhaps the most refreshing to God's people, and the most fruitful in the conversion of sinners. Some of his own people were there, and wishing for their fellow-parishioners the benefit which they themselves had derived, and expecting a renewal of their former enjoyment, they requested their minister to preach the same sermon at Resolis. He did so, but those who heard it before were this time greatly disappointed. Mentioning this to Mr M'Phail, he accounted for the difference by saying—"When in Petty, you were looking to the Lord, but in Resolis you were looking to me. There you got the manna fresh from heaven; here you got it after it had moulded in my memory."

On his death-bed, his hope of heaven was for a season sorely tried. Falling asleep in a dejected state of mind, he dreamt that he was waiting, lonely and despairing, outside the walls of the New Jerusalem. Seeing the gate closed, and none near to help him, and none in sight to cry to for help, he had just lain down to die, when he heard sounds as of a company approaching the city. Venturing to look up from the dust where he lay, he recognised Noah, Abraham, and all the patriarchs. As they drew near, the gate flew open, a glorious company from within came forth to meet them, and, in the midst of shouts of triumph, they entered. The gate again closes, and again he is left alone and hopeless. But soon he hears the noise of another company approaching. As they pass, he recognises Moses, Aaron, Samuel, David, and all the prophets, a glorious and a numerous band. Again the gate is thrown open, "an abundant entrance" given, and again he is left outside, and feels more desolate than ever. A third company is heard approaching composed of the Apostles and all the earliest Christians. They enter the city amidst rejoicing like the rest, and he, with less hope than ever, is still outside the gate. A fourth company now appears. Luther and Knox are at the head of those who form it. They pass him by like those who went before, are admitted into the city, and leave him alone and despairing without. Quite close to him now comes a fifth company. He recognises in it some of his friends and acquaintances, who had died in the Lord; but though their shining skirts touch him as they pass, he could not venture to arise and join them. Again he sees the gate open and close; and now, at last, he lays himself quite down to die. But he hears the footstep of a solitary pilgrim, coming exactly to the place where he lies. Looking up, he recognises Manasseh. Summoning all his strength, he takes hold of his skirt, as he moves slowly toward the city, and, creeping on behind him, he knows the gate has opened, by the light of the city's glory shining on his face; and just as he thought he heard the sound of the gate closing behind him, he suddenly awoke. The lesson of this dream was presented to him thereafter in the sweet words of Paul— "This is a faithful saying, and worthy of all acceptation, that Christ Jesus came into the world to save sinners, of whom I am chief."

His tombstone in the churchyard of Cullicudden bears the following inscription: "Here lies the body of the holy man of God and faithful minister of Jesus Christ, Mr Hector M'Phail, minister of the Gospel in this parish, who died 23rd January, 1774, aged fifty-eight years."

Four years before the death of Mr M'Phail, Mr Charles Calder[1] was ordained minister of Ferintosh. The Calders were a blessed race. Mr John Calder was minister of Cawdor from 1704 to 1717. His

[1]The succession of ministers in Ferintosh from the Revolution till Mr Calder was ordained on the 12th May, 1774:—

Andrew Ross, first a "Conform" minister or curate, was translated from Contin; admitted prior to 6th April, 1686; died in November, 1712; he is said to have been a very pious man and popular preacher.

Alexander Fraser, admitted 21st April, 1715; he was presented to the charge by John, Earl of Cromarty; translated to Inverness, 11th October, 1726.

Alexander Falconer was translated from Ardersier; admitted, 21st January, 1729; died, 8th April 1756, aged about 70, in the 38th year of his ministry; he was eminent both for piety and talents.

Donald Fraser, translated from Killearnan; admitted, 2nd June, 1757; died, 7th April, 1773, in his 67th year, and the 30th of his ministry. "He had a vigorous and comprehensive mind, and was possessed of extensive attainments; his chief delight was the good of his fellow-men. As a theologian he was profound, and in expounding the Scriptures had few equals. As a preacher he was clear and powerful, while his exhortations carried conviction with them to the conversion of many."

Charles Calder had his degree from the University and King's College, Aberdeen, in 1767; was licensed by the Presbytery of Inverness, 28th September, 1773; eminently devoted to his Master's service, few clergymen ever reigned more in the hearts of his people. — *Fasti Eccl. Scoti.*

gifts, his godliness, and his acceptance and success as a minister were such that throughout all the north he was known as "the great Mr Calder." His son, Mr James Calder, became minister of Ardersier in 1740, and about seven years thereafter was translated to Croy, where he died in 1775. Both as a Christian and a minister, he was no less eminent than his father. He had three sons — John, who was minister of Rosskeen, where his brief ministry was greatly blessed; Hugh, who succeeded his father, a talented and a godly man, but so delicate that he very seldom was able to preach; and Charles, the celebrated minister of Ferintosh.

Naturally amiable, with a vigorous intellect, refined taste, and more than ordinary accomplishments, under the sanctifying influence of the truth, Mr Charles Calder became "a man among a thousand." Early taught of God, and trained and guided by the discipline and example of his father, he came to his work as a minister with all the maturity which only long experience could give to another. Careful in his preparations for the pulpit, and much given unto prayer, he was not often seen abroad among his people; the stern call of duty alone drew him from his study. As a preacher he was quite singular; and it was his want of any marked peculiarity that made him so. His sermons were written with great care, but a chaste simplicity was the characteristic of his style. He seldom used an illustration; but all others would fail, when he did not succeed, in being sufficiently clear. His words were chosen not to please, but to instruct; and well chosen indeed they were, for his statements were so bathed in light, the words were never noticed. They were always so transparent, that the idea they contained was like a naked flame. His manner was chastened and quiet, but earnest and solemn. All was subordinated by him to the great end of setting only Christ before the eyes of sinners. His great theme was the love of Jesus. His own soul kept lying at the feet of Jesus; he was wont to give forth, with all the freshness of a present experience, his utterances regarding the person, love, death, and salvation of the blessed Redeemer. There never was a more affecting preacher, when discoursing on his favourite theme. Often have his whole congregation been in tears, as in his own tender, solemn way, he

commended Jesus as a Saviour to the lost; and when, with a
tremulous voice, but with the authority of one who knew he was
conveying a message from Jehovah, he warned the unbeliever of his
danger, the most indifferent were compelled to tremble. It was a
rare sight, to see that man of God, his meek face lighted with the
radiance of his humble joy, and his eyes suffused with tears, as he
poured out of the fulness of a contrite heart the praises of Christ
crucified, while many of his hearers were expressing by their
weeping, the influence which his doctrine had upon their hearts.
They were blessed Sabbaths these, in the church of Ferintosh.
Many a soul shall remember one of these days for ever, as "the
time of love," when the Lord first espoused him to Himself, and
when He cheered his heart as he was fainting on his journey
towards Zion.

He was not ignorant of Satan's devices. He was getting too near
to the mercy-seat to be allowed by the enemy to escape his revenge;
and he had, besides, to bear the malice which was provoked by the
inroads he was the means of making on his kingdom in the world.
Often did he find it difficult to leave his study on a Sabbath
morning, and many a sleepless Sabbath night did he spend, because
of the shortcomings of the Sabbath service. He had a partner of his
temporal lot, who was also a partner of his spiritual joys and
sorrows, and whose prudence was equal to her piety. Often to her
wise interference it was due that he went out at all to public duty.
Once she found him, in an agony of fear, lying on his study floor, at
the hour for beginning service in the church. "Oh, why was I ever
a minister?" he cried, as she entered; "I should have been a
tradesman rather." "My dear, the Lord knew that you had not the
strength for a tradesman's work," was his wife's wise reply, as she
pointed to his delicately formed limbs; "but, as He has given you a
voice wherewith to speak the praise of Christ, go with it to the work
which now awaits you." He rose and went to the pulpit; the Lord
shone on his soul, and blessed his preaching, and there are memories
in heaven, and will be for ever, of that Sabbath service in the
church of Ferintosh.

Having preached on the Monday of a communion season in

Dingwall a sermon, singular even among his own, so impressed were the souls of God's people by the doctrine, and so awed by the holy solemnity of the service, that none of them could venture to speak to him after it was over. His catechist was sitting beside the tent, and as Mr Calder was coming out of it he placed his hand on the steps by which the minister was descending, but was so overawed by what he had heard that he dared not to address him as he passed. It was not long when Satan began to retaliate on the Lord's servant for that day's work. The Tempter insisted that he had so grieved the hearts of God's people by that sermon that none of them would speak to him, and that even his catechist, Alexander Vass, was obliged, on that account, to turn his back upon him. Alexander expected that Satan would not allow his minister to pass scaithless after such a service, and in the evening of the next day he went to the manse. He was told, on entering, that the minister was ill, and Mrs Calder conducted him to her husband's bedroom. There he found his minister, in great distress, lying on his bed. Mr Calder told his state of mind, and how he had interpreted Alexander's conduct at the close of the service in Dingwall. The Catechist then informed him of the true state of feeling in which he and all the people of the Lord then present were at that time; and the snare of the fowler was broken.

His last illness was a short one. At its commencement he said to a Christian friend, "Here I am, like a ship at sea, without rudder, sail, or compass. If the Lord has said it, I will come, as a vessel of mercy, to the haven of glory; but if not, I am lost for ever." Shortly before his death he said, "I am content to lie here to the end of time, if the Lord would employ my suffering as the means of saving good to any one of my people." He entered into the joy of his Lord on the 1st of October, 1812.

Of all the eminent ministers in the Highlands, none is more famous than Mr Lachlan Mackenzie[1] of Lochcarron. Owing to his

[1]Lachlan Mackenzie was the son of the miller of Ord, Kilmuir-Wester, now Knockbain; studied at Marischal College and University of Aberdeen; became schoolmaster of Applecross; and was transferred to that of Lochcarron in 1776, and licensed by the Presbytery of Lochcarron, 4th October, 1780. He was

genius, his peculiar Christian experience, and his great acceptance as a preacher, he has retained a firmer hold of the memories of the people than any other besides. He was born in Kilmuir-Wester in 1754. Receiving an excellent classical education in his youth, and having a predilection for such studies, he attained to a considerable acquaintance with the dead languages, which he continued to retain, and even to extend, to the very evening of his life. He was only eight years of age when he first felt the saving power of the truth, and he became distinguished at once for his devotion to prayer, which was his great peculiarity during all his subsequent life. A few years before he was licensed, he was appointed parish schoolmaster of Lochcarron. The majority of the Presbytery were not disposed to forward the views of a youth who showed such marked symptoms of the religious enthusiasm, which was regarded as a plague in the last century by the stipend-lifters of the Establishment. Men who thought that to earn a stipend it was enough to read a borrowed sermon on Sabbath, and that, after spending so unpleasant an hour in the church, they had a right to enjoy all the other hours of the week at their ease in the manse, were not likely to look with favour on the schoolmaster who set up prayer-meetings and who ventured to read the Bible and to expound it to the people at most uncanonical hours. They resolved, therefore, to withhold licence from Mr Lachlan. In point of scholarship and theology he was ahead of all his judges, but merely because he could not be kept from praying they were determined to keep him from preaching. They agreed, at last, to licence him on condition of his not being settled within their own bounds, a promise to that effect having

promoted to the Mission of Uist, which he demitted, and, renouncing certain wild notions he had entertained in religion, was presented by George III, 9th October, 1781, and ordained 4th April, 1782. He stated in 1811 that 232 of his parishioners could read English, only 2 were capable of reading Gaelic, while no fewer than 645 could read neither language, exclusive of children. He died 20th April, 1819, in the 66th year of his age, and the 38th of his ministry. "Simplicity of manners presented in him a picture of apostolic times, whose heavenliness of mind spurned objects of time and sense, while his imagination shed a bright lustre on every subject which he handled, and the unction in his ministrations endeared him to his people."

been given by the patron. But his chief opponents in the Presbytery were removed soon after, and his settlement at Lochcarron took place in 1782, and there he continued to labour till his death.

His immediate predecessor was Mr Donald Munro. "He was an agreeable man, and preached the Gospel in its purity," is Mr Lachlan's account of him — a tribute not kept back by recollections of his unkind treatment of himself when he was pursuing his studies for the ministry. Unable to appreciate his schoolmaster, and regarding his eccentricity as a proof of his being below and not above the average of intellectual power, he had always dissuaded Mr Lachlan from aspiring to the ministry, and refused him all aid against his enemies in the Presbytery.

Mr Munro was preceded by the famous Mr Aeneas Sage — "a man of an undaunted spirit, who did not know what the fear of man was. He had, however, the fear of God, and great zeal for the good cause in its highest perfection. He was the determined enemy of vice, and a true friend of the gospel." Such, according to Mr Lachlan, was the character of Mr Sage, the first minister who is known to have preached the Gospel in purity and with success in Lochcarron. At the time of his induction, the state of the parish was very much the same as it was found by the Presbytery to be in 1649, when, after visiting it, they reported "there were no elders in it by reason of malignancy; swearing, drunkenness, cursing, Sabbath profanation, and uncleanness prevailed." As to the church, there was found in it "ane formal stool of repentance, but no pulpit nor desks." The stool, if the only, was truly the suitable seat for all the people of Lochcarron in those days; but the more it was required, the less power there was to make it aught else than "ane formal" thing, as the solitary occupant of the church.

Matters continued in this state till the induction of Mr Sage, nearly eighty years after. He was just the man for the work of breaking up the fallow ground of a field so wild, and a rich blessing rested on his labours. On the night of his first arrival at Lochcarron an attempt was made to burn the house in which he lodged, and for some time after his induction his life was in constant danger. But the esteem he could not win as a minister, he soon acquired for his great physical strength. The first man in Lochcarron in those days was the champion at the athletic games. Conscious of his strength, and knowing that he would make himself respected by all if he could only lay big Rory on his back, who was acknowledged to be the strongest man in the district, the minister joined the people on the earliest opportunity at their games. Challenging the whole field, he competed for the prize in putting the stone, tossing the caber, and wrestling, and won an easy victory. His fame was established at once. The minister was now the champion of the district, and none was more ready to defer to him than he whom he had deprived of the laurel. Taking Rory aside to a confidential crack, he said to him, "Now, Rory, I am the minister, and you must be my elder, and we both must see to it that all the people attend church, observe the Sabbath, and conduct themselves properly." Rory fell in with the proposal at once. On Sabbath, when the people would gather at their games in the forenoon, the minister and his elder would join them, and each taking a couple by the hand, they would drag them to the church, lock them in, and then return to catch some more. This was repeated till none were left on the field. Then, stationing the elder with his cudgel at the door, the minister would mount the pulpit and conduct the service. One of his earliest sermons was blessed to the conversion of his assistant, and a truly valuable coadjutor he found in big Rory thereafter. Mr Lachlan thus describes the result of his ministry: "Mr Sage made the people very orthodox." They "seem to have a strong attachment to religion." "There is a great appearance of religion in Lochcarron; and as the fire of God's Word is hereafter to try every man's work, there is cause to hope that some of it will bear the trial."

Such was the state of Lochcarron at the time of Mr Lachlan's induction. Taught to respect a godly minister, the people cordially welcomed Mr Lachlan as their pastor. His fame as a Christian was already great; they had experience of his gifts as a speaker; and he occupied, at once, the place of an approved ambassador of Christ in the regards of the people.

He was of a peculiarly sensitive temperament, rendering him susceptible of the deepest impressions. Were it not for his powerful intellect, he would have been the creature of impulse, driven by his feelings rather than guided by his judgment. It is seldom so much mind and heart are found in one man. The light of a heartless intellectualism, or the fire of an impulsive sentimentalism, are often the alternatives in the case of those who have risen above the crowd. But, in him, the clear head and the warm heart were connected. Capable of forming a vivid conception of a subject, his imagination never failed to furnish him with metaphors by which aptly to illustrate it. He was no poet, though he often rhymed; but, if he could not form those pleasing combinations of natural objects, which, by their novelty and beauty, attest the working of poetic genius, he had the power of tracing analogies between the things of intellect and the things of sense. This, to a preacher, is the most useful endowment, and the imagination is more safely employed in such an office, than when scattering the gems of poesy over the treasures of truth.

His Christian experience was singular. Early taught to know the Lord, one would have expected his course to have been unusually even. But the very reverse was the case; for few Christians ever experienced such marked changes of feeling. Now on the brink of despair under the power of temptation, and soon again in a state of rapturous enjoyment, shade and sunshine alternated in abrupt and rapid succession, during the whole of his life. Ardent and imaginative as he was, the fiery darts of the wicked one flashed the more vividly, and pierced the more deeply into his soul, and the joy that came to him from heaven the more violently excited him. His prayerfulness was the leading feature of his Christianity. Much of his time was spent on his knees, and many a sleepless night he passed, sometimes wrestling, as for his life, against the assaults of the tempter, and at other times "rejoicing in the hope of the glory of God." The nearness to the mercy seat, to which he was sometimes admitted, was quite extraordinary. Proofs of this might be given, because of which we cannot wonder that he had the fame and the influence of a prophet, among the simple people of the north, but the record of which would cause most incredulous nodding of the wise heads of the south. Avoiding the extreme of a superstitious credulity, on the one hand, and of the formalist's scepticism, on the other, it is altogether safe to say that Mr Lachlan enjoyed peculiarly familiar intercourse with God, and received such distinct intimations of His mind, in reference to the cases which he carried to the mercy-seat, as but very few of God's children have obtained.

His preaching was always remarkable. His great originality of thought and manner, his apt and striking illustrations, his clear and emphatic utterance, the unction and authority with which he spake, his close dealing with the conscience, his dexterous and tender handling of the case of the tempted, his powerful appeals, his solemn earnestness, and his frequent outbursts of impassioned feeling, could not fail to win for him a measure of acceptance, as they gave him a measure of power beyond that of any other of his brethren. His was preaching to which all could listen with interest. His striking illustrations, often homely, though always apt, would arrest the attention of the most ignorant and careless. There was an intellectual treat in his sermons for such as could appreciate the efforts of genius. The scoffer was arrested and awed by the authority with which he spoke, and every hearer seeking the bread of life hung upon his lips. A congregation was always eager to hear when Mr Lachlan was to preach. A large crowd once gathered in Killearnan to hear him. So many had assembled that the church could not contain them, and the service was conducted in the open air. When the text was announced, a rude fellow, sitting in the outskirts of the congregation, called out in the excitement of his eagerness, ''Speak out; we cannot hear.'' Mr Lachlan, not disconcerted in the least, raised his voice and said, ''My text is, 'Ye have need of patience,'" which the man no sooner heard than he was fain to hold his tongue and hide his face with shame.

The minuteness with which he described the feelings and habits of his hearers, and the striking confirmation of his doctrine, often given by the Lord in His providence, gave him an extraordinary influence over his people. Preaching on one occasion against the sin of lying, he counselled his people to refrain, in all circumstances, from prevarication and falsehood, assuring them that they would find it their best policy for time, as well as their safest course for eternity. One of his hearers, conscious of having often told a lie, and finding it impossible to believe that it could always be wise to tell the truth, went to speak to the minister on the subject. He was a smuggler, and while conversing with Mr Lachlan, he said, "Surely, if the exiseman should ask me where I hid my whisky, it would not be wrong that I should lead him 'off the scent.'" His minister would not allow this was a case to which the rule he laid down was not applicable, and advised him, even in such circumstances, to tell the simple truth. The smuggler was soon after put to the test. While working behind his house by the wayside, on the following week, the exciseman came up to him and said, "Is there any whisky about your house to-day?" Remembering his minister's advice, the smuggler at once said, though not without misgivings as to the result, "Yes, there are three casks of whisky buried in a hole under my bed, and if you will search for them there you will find them." "You rascal," the exciseman said, "if they were there you would be the last to tell me"; and at once walked away. As soon as he was out of hearing, and the smuggler could breathe freely again, he exclaimed, "Oh, Mr Lachlan, Mr Lachlan, you were right as usual!"

On another occasion he was bearing testimony against dishonest dealing, assuring his hearers that sooner or later the Lord would punish all who held the balances of deceit. As an example of how the Lord sometimes, even in this life, gives proof of His marking the sin of dishonesty, he repeated an anecdote which was current at the time. A woman, who had been engaged in selling milk, with which she always mingled a third of water, and who had made some money by her traffic, was going with her gains to America. During the voyage she kept her treasure in a bag which was always under her pillow. There was a monkey on board the ship, that was allowed to go at large, and that in course of its wanderings came to the milkwoman's hammock, in rummaging which it found the bag of gold. Carrying it off, the monkey mounted the rigging, and, seating itself aloft on a spar, opened the bag and began to pick out the coins. The first it threw out into the sea, and the second and third it dropped on the deck, and so on, till a third of all the contents of the bag had sunk in the ocean, the owner of the bag being allowed to gather off the deck just what she had fairly earned by her milk. One of Mr Lachlan's hearers remembered, while listening to this anecdote, that he had in his trunk at home a bundle of banknotes, which he had got by the sale of diluted whisky. Feeling very uneasy, he hurried to his house after the sermon was over. It was dark before he arrived, and, kindling a pine torch, he hastened to the place where he kept his money, afraid that it had been taken away. Holding the torch with one hand, while he turned over the notes with the other, a flaming ember fell right down into the midst of his treasure, and before the man, bewildered as he was, could rescue them, as many of the notes were consumed as exactly represented the extent to which he had diluted the whisky.

Never did a sudden death occur in the parish, during his ministry, without some intimation of it being given from the pulpit on the previous Sabbath; and sometimes warnings would be so strikingly verified that one cannot wonder he was regarded as a prophet by his people. Such instances of the minute guidance of the Lord could not fail to make a deep impression on a simple-minded people, and should not fail to make some impression on any people.

The most famous sermon he ever preached was on "the Babe in Bethlehem." It made a very deep impression on the minds of such of the Lord's people as were privileged to hear it; and the memories of that sermon were always recalled with peculiar vividness and delight. The preacher having proposed to go to seek for Jesus, an inquirer was supposed to offer to attend him, and the two were represented as setting out together on the search. They had not got far, when, the inquirer's eye resting on a fine house not far away, he said, "Surely this is the place where we will find Him." "Come, and let us see," was the guide's reply. They go to the fine mansion, and peeping in through the window, they see a company seated round a gaming table. "Oh, come away, come away; Jesus cannot be here," the inquirer cries. "I knew that," his guide replied, "but while we are on the way to some other place, let me tell you what will be the fate of the company on which we were looking." He then detailed the future of the family in the mansion, and the programme he gave was exactly carried out, in the after-history of a family in his parish. ''Oh, perhaps he is there,'' says the inquirer, pointing to another house. ''Come, and let us see,'' was again the guide's reply. They reached the house, but they had only just stood, when the hoarse laugh of the drunkard sounded in their ears. Again the inquirer is satisfied that they must seek elsewhere for Jesus; and, again, with wonderful minuteness, the minister describes the future career of another household in his parish. After repeated trials, made at his own suggestion, the inquirer begins to despair of finding Jesus at all. He leaves himself now entirely in the hands of his guide, who brings him to the back court of the inn, and, pointing to the door of the stable, says, ''It is there Jesus will be found.'' ''There!'' cries the inquirer, ''behind that mass of filth,'' as he pointed to the dung-heap at the door of the stable. Applying this to his remembrance of past sins, and his fear that one so guilty as he could never find Jesus, the guide reasoned with the inquirer till his first difficulty was removed. He then brings him to the threshold, but the filth within now arrests him. ''Oh, surely,'' he cries, ''he cannot be in such a place as this.'' Applying this to his sense of indwelling corruption, his guide again reasons with the inquirer till his second difficulty is removed. But seeing beasts within, he is afraid to cross over to the manger. This suggests the presence and wiles of the tempter, and the inquirer's fears, arising from temptation, are met and removed. At last the manger is reached, and there, in swaddling clothes, they find the infant Jesus. In the renewed will of the inquirer himself, seeking Christ as revealed and offered in the Gospel, and as he fain would embrace Him in the promise, if he dare, Jesus at last is found, notwithstanding all past guilt, abounding corruption, and harassing temptations.

Mr Lachlan was very careful in his preparation for the pulpit, though it was only when his mental vigour was declining that he began to write his discourses. The few specimens of these which have been given to the public furnish no adequate idea of his preaching. His illustrations were never written, and the published skeletons are the productions of his later years, when his power was on the wane.

His last service in public was an address to communicants at the table of the Lord. He was then unable to stand without support. The minister of Killearnan, seating himself at the head of the table, with Mr Lachlan standing in front of him, held him up with his strong arms from behind. Mustering all his strength, he poured out with his broken voice, from a broken heart, the praises of redeeming love.

A stroke of paralysis laid him prostrate during the last year of his life. Mind and body alike succumbed to the blow, and, before the year had closed, the friends who loved him best were willing that he should leave them to enter on the rest for which his soul was pining. It required such a visitation as this to reconcile them to his death. He had survived his usefulness to the Church on earth, and there was now no inducement to wish him longer ''absent from the Lord.''

The following appropriate inscription, composed by Dr Ross, of Lochbroom, is engraved on his humble tombstone: ''Here are deposited the mortal remains of the Rev. Lachlan Mackenzie, late minister of Lochcarron, who died April 20th, 1819, in the 37th year of his ministry. A man whose simplicity of manners presented a picture of apostolic times; whose heavenliness of mind still spurned the vain objects of time and sense; whose vivid imagination shed a bright lustre on every subject which he handled; and whose holy unction in all his ministrations endeared him to the people of God, and embalmed his memory in their hearts. His praise is in the churches. His parish mourns.''

Mr Macadam's[1] first charge was the Gaelic congregation of Cromarty. His ministry there was greatly blessed — more so, perhaps, than it ever was in the parish of Nigg, to which he was

---

[1]Alexander Macadam was schoolmaster of Cromarty; licensed by the Presbytery of Chanonry, 4th May, 1779; was called, 18th June, 1781, to the Little Church or Chapel of Ease, Elgin, and supplied till promoted to the Gaelic Chapel, Cromarty, to which he was presented by George III in March, and ordained, 25th September, 1782. He was promoted from the Gaelic Chapel,

translated, and in which he laboured till his death. The intrusion of his predecessor had driven many of the people of Nigg out of the Establishment, and a congregation was formed, and a church built, in the parish, in connection with the Secession. The minister of that charge, in Mr Macadam's day, was Mr Buchanan, a godly man, who was greatly beloved and respected by his people. For some time Mr Macadam and he kept very much aloof from each other, but a circumstance occurred which was the occasion of bringing them, during their latter years, more closely together. Mr Macadam, having been sent for, to visit one of his hearers who was dying, went to the house, but on reaching the door, was arrested by a passage of Scripture which was applied with peculiar power to his heart, in the face of which not daring to enter, he turned away and went home. The relatives of the dying man were greatly offended, and immediately sent for Mr Buchanan; but his conduct was an exact repetition of that of the parish minister. Mr Macadam, hearing this, visited Mr Buchanan, and was surprised to find that the very same passage which had arrested himself was suggested to him also, and had made the self-same impression on his mind. This helped them to discover that they were more at one than their relative positions seemed to indicate. Mr Macadam thereafter compared himself and Mr Buchanan to two men engaged in thatching the same house though on opposite sides. These thatchers, as their work proceeded, would approach each other, till, when their work was finished, they would meet together at the top. The ministers thus recognised each other as fellow-labourers about the house of the Lord, though they seemed to be opposed, expecting to meet together, and be for ever with the Lord, when their work on earth was done.

As a preacher, Mr Macadam was peculiarly acceptable to the people of God. To his solemn and weighty thoughts he gave expression in terse vigorous words, fitly uttered with a deep sonorous voice. His sermons were remarkably compact and powerful,

Cromarty, to be parish minister of Nigg; presented to this charge by George III in March, and admitted 22nd October, 1788; died, 8th June, 1817, in his 69th year, and the 35th of his ministry, having been an eminent and learned theologian.

containing a luminous statement of doctrine, aptly illustrated and skilfully applied.

A note of his preaching, often quoted by Dr Macdonald, deserves to be remembered: "Why are there so many bankrupt professors of religion in our day? It is because they start without a capital."

During the latter years of his life he devoted much time to the study of unfulfilled prophecy, and his case furnishes a striking proof of how dangerous that study is. Few men possessed a more solid judgment than he, and yet his views of unfulfilled prophecy were so extravagant and confused, that all his judiciousness, so remarkable in other departments, seemed to have forsaken him when he entered upon this. Many cruder and more confused charts of the future may have been drawn since his day, but these came generally from hands that were never known to be under the guidance of a sober judgment. The study of prophecy has now become the fashionable religious diversion, and it is no wonder that those should be drawn aside after it, who were never strongly attached to the fundamental doctrines of the Gospel, and have never clearly seen, firmly held, and deeply felt them. But if even the godly and judicious Macadam wandered into tangled mazes there, sure indeed of guidance from on high ought anyone to be who feels disposed to follow him into the field of prophecy.

His most intimate friend, of all his brethren in the Presbytery, was Mr Kennedy of Logie. There was ever between them both the closest Christian fellowship, while together on the earth, and often have they enjoyed a sweet foretaste of the converse with each other, and of the communion with the Lord, which now fill their hearts with gladness in the "Father's house." Mr Macadam died on the eighth day of June, 1817, in the sixty-ninth year of his age.

Dr Angus Mackintosh[1] was minister of a Gaelic chapel in Glasgow before his removal to Tain. His preaching in Glasgow drew around him, as his stated hearers, the pious Highlanders in the

[1]Angus Mackintosh, promoted from the Gaelic Chapel, Glasgow; presented by George III in March, and by Isabel, Lady Elibank, same month, and admitted 11th May, 1797; had D.D. from the University and King's College, Aberdeen, 19th April, 1823; and died 3rd October, 1831, in the 68th year of

city, and many of the Lord's people from the surrounding country, and from neighbouring towns, used occasionally to repair to his church. Blessed to many were his labours then. In 1797 he was translated to Tain, and his ministry there, which at once won the confidence and attachment of the godly, and was commended to the consciences of all, continued to the end to maintain its acceptance and its power.

His personal appearance was remarkable. Tall and of a massive figure, a dark complexion, a face full of expression, and a bearing peculiarly solemn and dignified, he attracted at once the eye of a stranger, and never failed to command his respect. Those who knew him well could tell what kind of subject he had been studying, from the expression of his countenance as he entered the pulpit. The text had been deeply and powerfully affecting his heart, and his expressive face gave out the feeling which it had produced. There was a gloom of awe on his countenance, as if the very shadow of Sinai were darkening it, when his heart was charged with a message of terror; and the softened cast of his features, and the gleam of light in his eye, at other times, encouraged the broken-hearted to expect a message of encouragement and comfort.

To a stranger he seemed to wear an air of sternness. His love did not lie on the surface, like that of many, whose indiscriminate kindliness is seen by every eye, while they have no hidden treasures of affection for any. His heart once reached, it was found fraught with love; but it was too precious and too sanctified to be given in intimate fellowship to any but to those whom he could embrace as brethren in Christ. Those who loved him at all, loved him as they loved no other. In the society of kindred spirits there was often a radiant cheerfulness in his manner that made his conversation peculiarly attractive. But he was the man of God wherever he was, ever keeping an unflinching front to sin. His holy life, and the authority of his doctrine, and his solemn and dignified bearing, invested him with a power before which iniquity hid its face, and

his age, and the 39th of his ministry. He was secretary to the Northern Missionary Society, and one of its originators. He married, 6th June, 1800, Anne, youngest daughter of the Rev. Charles Calder, Urquhart, who survived him until 23rd January, 1857.

evil-doers could not be bold to sin. How precious to a country is the influence of such a life and of such a ministry as his! Alas! how rare is such a blessing now. May the Lord have mercy on the people who have sinned it away!

His impressions of divine things were peculiarly solemn, his convictions of sin had been unusually deep, and his views of the way of salvation uncommonly clear and decided. "Knowing the terror of the Lord," as few besides have known it, overpoweringly urgent was his way of persuading the sinner to flee from "the wrath to come." He was, indeed, "a son of thunder," in preaching the law to the Christless, and seared must have been the conscience of the man who could listen to him without fear; but, at the same time, no preacher could be more careful not to hurt when the Lord was healing. At the close of one of his solemn and searching discourses, under which none seemed to be spared, and all hopes seemed to be levelled in the dust, carefully would he search out the cases of the "poor in spirit," and speak comfort to "the broken in heart." In unravelling the mystery of iniquity and in exposing all counterfeits of godliness he was peculiarly solemn and skilful; and when unfolding and applying the doctrines of grace there was an unction, a clearness, and a power in his preaching to which very few have attained.

Looking back, from his death-bed, on his experience as a preacher, he said: "I have had days of darkness in the pulpit; but I have felt, at other times, while preaching Christ to sinners, as if I were already in heaven."

Walking in his garden, shortly before his death, leaning on the arm of his son, he stopped at a certain spot, each time he made a circuit on the walk around it. Standing, for the third or fourth time, in the same place, he pointed to a withered tree hard by. "There am I, Charles," he said, and then burst into tears. How touching a proof of his deep self-abasement before God! How ready was this faithful servant of the Lord to count himself unprofitable after all he had done, and how willing to acknowledge, that if he ever entered into the joy of the Lord, it must be as "the chief of sinners" saved by grace! He died in October, 1831, in the sixty-eighth year of his age and in the thirty-ninth of his ministry.

Mr William Forbes[1] of Tarbat was Dr Mackintosh's most intimate friend. They had been companions, as pupils in the Fortrose Academy and as students in King's College, Aberdeen; and the warm attachment, then formed, knew no interruption during all their subsequent intercourse.

If kindliness of manner is required to make a man amiable, Mr Forbes was far from being so. There was a rough crust on the outside of him, but there was much sterling love beneath it, though too deep for all to find it. With a horror of affectation, a rigid exactness of habits, a contempt of petty conventionalities, and an eruptive temper, there was not much about him to attract the affection of those who would not love him for his godliness. Sometimes he would unbend, when softened by the genial intercourse of Christian friends, and on such occasions he infused so much genuine humour into his conversation, that one wondered where he usually hid the stores on which he then drew so largely. A man of sterling worth he was, who could afford to want the smooth exterior that other men require to make them tolerable. Always holding his best in reserve, one could never duly value him who did not know him thoroughly. He bore to be examined, and the longer and closer one's intercourse with him was the more he commanded his affection and respect. Unscared by the fear of man, he was an unsparing reprover of sin wherever it appeared. Not accessible to the impressions by which others might be swayed from following the strict requirements of conscience, he kept his flock invariably under the strictest discipline. But no man was less disposed to lord it

[1] Mr William Forbes was promoted from the Gaelic Chapel, Aberdeen; presented by Mrs Henrietta Gordon of Newhall, and admitted 24th April, 1800; departed, 12th May, 1838, in the 72nd year of his age, and the 48th of his ministry. He was almost the last — *ultimus Romanorum* — of a cluster of venerable men whose systematic and able exposition of doctrine, personal piety, talent, and consistency of life and conversation, gladdened and benefited "the people's poor ones, and the children of the needy," elevated the tone of religious profession, as well as the ministerial office, and drew around themselves and their ministrations the estimation and confidence of the good and the excellent of their day and generation. He married, 26th November, 1813, Jane, youngest daughter of the Rev. Alexander Sage of Kildonan, who departed 29th December, 1852.

over the consciences of his people, while careful to keep his own "void of offence," in his dealings with them all. The result of this stern regime was an order and propriety in the demeanour of his congregation in the house of God, such as could not elsewhere be found.

His clear and vigorous intellect, with a cultivated taste, enabled him to clothe in most expressive language the exactest thinking. He was scrupulously careful in his preparation for the pulpit. His manuscripts were often quite as ready for the press as for the pulpit, though they never found their way to either. As a lecturer there have been few to excel him; and at the head of a communion table, where he opened up, as on no other occasion, the rich treasures of his experience, his addresses were peculiarly refreshing to the people of the Lord. Solemn and quiet in his manner, and most emphatic in his utterance, he spoke with such authority and unction as never failed to command the attention of his hearers. Precious to God's people have his sermons often been, and by his hand has the Lord sent the arrow of conviction to not a few proud hearts. He died in May, 1838. His ministry in Tarbat began in the first year of the century.

The last of the great Ross-shire Fathers who passed into his rest was, in some respects, the first. The extent of his labours, and his great popularity and success, won for him the name of "the apostle of the north." More in the eye of the public, the name of Dr Macdonald [1] is familiar to many, to whom those of some of the others are utterly unknown. His was mainly the work of an evangelist; and his great physical energy, his masculine intellect, his retentive memory, his buoyancy of spirits, his pleasant manner, the fervour of his love, and the character of his Christian experience, marked him out as an instrument of the Lord's own fashioning for the work in which he was engaged. A more extended memoir of his life and labours being in course of preparation, it is unnecessary to anticipate here the record that may yet be given.

[1] John M'Donald was promoted from the Gaelic Chapel, Edinburgh; admitted 1st September, 1813; had D.D. from the University of New York; departed, 16th April, 1849, in his 70th year, and the 43rd of his ministry.

The "fathers, where are they?" "Woe is me! For I am as when they have gathered the summer fruits, as the grape gleanings of the vintage; there is no cluster to eat; my soul desired the first-ripe fruit."

CHAPTER III

"THE MEN" OF ROSS-SHIRE

"THE MEN" were so named not because they were not women, but because they were not ministers. It was necessary to distinguish between the ministers and the other speakers at a fellowship meeting, when notes of their addresses were given; and the easiest way of doing so was by saying "one of the ministers" or "one of the men said so." Hence the origin of the designation; and speakers at religious meetings in the Highlands, who are not ministers, are those to whom it is applied.

An unfavourable opinion is entertained of them by some, because they know them not; but an unfair representation has been given of them by others, because they liked them not. Not a few have been accustomed to speak of "the men," whom perhaps it would not be impossible to persuade that, if they caught a live specimen, he would be found to have both horns and hoofs. The name presents to some minds a class of proud, turbulent fellows, who will submit to no rule, and are always in a state of mutiny against all ecclesiastical authority. The idea of "the men," in other minds, is that they are a set of superstitious and bigoted persons, who see visions and who dream dreams, and who think that their own straitened circle encloses all the vital Christianity on the earth. Nor have there been awanting those who would denounce them as mystics in their religion, and as antinomians in their practice. It is trying to have to notice these gross misrepresentations when one looks back on the noble phalanx of worthies to whom they have been applied; but it is a relief to remember that those who have spoken "all manner of evil against them falsely" have but unwittingly proved that "the men" were a people whom the Lord had blessed.

To various sources may be traced the prevalence of these mistaken estimates of the men. There is an anti-Highland feeling that is apt to prejudice unconsciously the Lowlander against them, just because they speak in Gaelic and are peculiar to the north. His incapacity to judge, owing to his ignorance of what may be said in Gaelic, and of what may suit the north, does not prevent his attempting to judge notwithstanding. Conscious of superiority, it is difficult for him to believe that what he cannot appreciate can possibly be good. Men will try to form a positive judgment regarding all they think to be beneath themselves, and when they are compelled to feel that they cannot intelligently do so, they are very prone to vent their mortification in sweeping censures or in expressions of contempt.

Not unfrequent have been references to "the men" and their ways in a tourist's sketches of the Highlands; and however unjust his verdict might have been, and however impossible it was that he could have accurately described them, he found many who would both read and receive his opinions about them. In the uncivilised north everything must, of course, lie within the ken of a wise man from the south, and the order, influence, and habits of "the men," with all else that may come in his way. He may have lighted on the place where a congregation met on the Friday of a communion season. Asking why the people were assembled, he would be told they were engaged in public worship. Curiosity would arrest him for a time on the outskirts of the crowd. He sees one man after another rise up to speak, and he listens, with amused attention, to the strange guttural sounds which they emit. Remembering the service in a Cathedral in which he worshipped a few days before, what a contrast to its pompous ritual is presented in the scene before him! The bishop in his lawn, the altar, the organ, and the choir, the chanted liturgy, and the well-delivered sermon, the fine attire, and the graceful genuflections of the people who surrounded him, as he sat in his well-cushioned pew, all rise up in his memory; and who can wonder that he smiles with supreme contempt on all the actors and ongoings, and, excepting of course, his own presence, all the circumstances of the scene before him. Betaking himself to his desk, on his return from the place where he saw it, he would thus describe the hill-side gathering: "I walked about after breakfast to-day, and lighted on a strange scene. A large crowd of men and women were seated in a shaded hollow on the hillside, engaged in public worship, after the grotesque fashion of the Highlands. There were two or three of their parsons confined in a wooden box at one side of the congregation, as if the people had shut them in there, in order to take their own way of conducting the service. Their own way they indeed seemed to have, for I saw one man after another rise up among the crowd, each of them with long hair down to his shoulder, and a huge cloak down to his heels, and with a handkerchief wrapped round his head; and there they successively stood, uttering the strangest sounds through their noses, with as much solemnity and earnestness as if they were delivering the most edifying discourses. 'Like priest like people,' is true in the Highlands as elsewhere, for their hearers seemed quite as earnest, because quite as witless as themselves. Losing all patience at last, I turned away and left them."

Let us suppose one of the worshippers whom he saw on the hillside returning the tourist's visit, and, after having been on a Sabbath in his grand cathedral, giving an account of what he saw. How would he describe what he saw? "I entered," he would say, "a large building that seemed made for any purpose but that of hearing, with windows daubed over with paint, as if those who made them were afraid the light of heaven would come pure on the people who might meet within. There were a great many strange things inside that seemed made on purpose to be looked at, and to keep the eyes of sinners on mere wood and stone. I was not long seated when in stalked a man who seemed to have come straight from his bed, for he had on his nightgown, which fortunately happened to be a long one. The poor man must have been crazy, for who in his senses would have come in such a plight before a congregation. Turning towards the people he began to read some gibberish out of a book, but what was my astonishment to see the people attending to what the poor creature was muttering, and kneeling as if they were praying along with him. All of a sudden he and they rose from their knees, and there came a sound like that of a pipe and fiddle together from behind me. I thought when I heard the music begin that the people had risen up to dance; but no, they stood quite still. On looking round I saw, instead of a pipe and fiddle, a large box with long yellow whistles stuck in the front of it, from which came the noise. The deluded people, it seems, as they did not like to praise the Lord themselves, and were afraid not to get it done at all, set this box to make a noise through its whistles for them. But, by this time, I had more than enough of it; and, remembering it was the Lord's Day, I hurried out of the place, right glad to escape from the synagogue of Satan.''

Such would, probably, be the simple Highlander's account of the cathedral and its service; but it would be quite as faithful as the tourist's description of the fellowship meeting in the north. But the latter can write letters from the Highlands which will appear in print, and which will be read and believed; and he has thus succeeded in giving such an impression of ''the men'' to many, that they always rise up before their mind's eye in long cloaks and with long hair, and with a napkin on their heads, pouring, in a rough stream of gutterals, nonsensical cant through their noses, over a crowd of gaping barbarians.

But to strangers cannot be traced all the falsehoods spoken and written of ''the men.'' They had bitter enemies at home, in the ungodly ministers of many Highland parishes. These they would not hear, and their influence secured to them a following when they went to other places to hear the gospel. This was the only thing these ministers could urge as a reason for opposing them. But all the more virulent was their enmity, because ''they could find none occasion nor fault'' against them, ''excepting concerning the law of'' their ''God.'' As no manner of evil could be spoken against them truly, all the more ready were they to speak ''all manner of evil against'' them ''falsely.'' Abuse of ''the men'' was sure to be mingled, in due proportion, with the copious after-dinner libations of every party of Moderates. Some of them never appeared in print but when they published a tirade against ''the men,'' and never rose in a Church court except to deliver an elaborate invective against them. In the measure in which they could give wing to their calumnies against these troublers of the peace, they succeeded in circulating false opinions regarding them.

"The Veto Act" brought out against "the men" the malice of another class of enemies. Preachers, who had been trained with a view to stipend-lifting, began to feel that the influence of "the men" intercepted them from "the loaves and fishes." They felt it hard that they could not live and preach as they listed, without endangering the prospect of a settlement, and that these "Gileadites took the passages" before them, and had "their senses exercised to discern" that "they could not frame to pronounce" the "Shibboleth." A loud blast against them has been sounded by an Ephraimite whom they scared from the north. Confining attention to a coterie in Caithness, as distinct from "the men" of Ross-shire in their faults as they were in other respects from himself, he offers a caricature of their failings as a description of all "the men" of the north. This was "Investigator's" form of attack, strong only in its malignity, though he assumed the airs of a victor, and found a lawyer who would write his pæan in the "Quarterly." His panegyrist is well known, and it is easy to determine under whose banner he fought, when the hand is discovered that gave him the laurel. But, louder than all the praises of his prowess, shall yet sound in his ears, the voice that from heaven proclaimeth — "Woe unto that man by whom offences come."

There have been, in the north, for half-a-century at least, a few cliques of Separatists, quite distinct from the order of "the men." Specimens of the former have often been taken as if fairly representing the latter. Among these Separatists were men of eminent piety, and some of eminent gifts. Disgusted by the ungodliness, or driven off by the tyranny, of Moderate ministers, they separated from the Church, and assumed an almost distinct position to themselves. Having begun to be leaders, in the first consciousness of power, they were unduly elated, and became the censors of some of whom they should have been the disciples. Some followed them, who had all their exclusiveness, with but little of their piety, and with none of their prudence. Sheltering themselves under the acknowledged godliness of their leaders, they became bold in their bitterness, and indiscriminate in their censures, against the good and the bad, among those with whom they had parted. Some of them became leaders in their turn, and though very different from the worthies, whose place they assumed, they failed not to secure a following of adherents. Extreme specimens of this section of the Separatists might be found, who used an extravagant profession as a covering over much pride and worldliness of heart, and some licentiousness of practice. But these could not be taken as fair specimens, even of the Separatists, and were no specimens at all of "the men."

It would be a reproach on the memory of such a man as the godly John Grant, to accept, as his fitting successors, some who seized upon his mantle after he was gone. A godly man, and blameless in his life was he, and much might be said to account for, if not to excuse, the exclusiveness by which he stinted his comfort and straitened his sympathies, and for which he himself, ere he died, expressed his regret. More gifted, but less godly than John Grant, was the famous Sandy Gair. Less watchful than the other, he was a Christian notwithstanding, and was decidedly a man of genius. No one, able to appreciate talent, could listen to one of his addresses without admiring the originality of his views, and the clear terseness of his diction. In apt illustration, and in scathing satire, few could excel him. Twice only did the writer ever hear him, but one of his sayings he cannot forget. Speaking of the advantage possessed by the Christian over the worldly in the security of his portion, he said, "It was not much that Jacob took with him when he left the house of Laban to return to his kindred, but amidst the little which he brought away, Laban lost his gods; but though Satan stripped Job till he left not even his skin on him, the patriarch still could say, 'I know that my Redeemer liveth.'" Speaking, on another occasion, of the very different estimates of their respective services formed by the Christian and the hypocrite, he said "Of the offering accepted on Mount Carmel, the fire from heaven left only the ashes to Elijah; but, had the priests of Baal survived, they might have fed themselves fat on their rejected sacrifice."

But in Ross-shire at no period were there many of the class now referred to, nor did the few who were, attain to a name and an influence that make it necessary to notice them. This is accounted for by the fact that there was a succession of ministers there who commanded the respect of all classes of the people, and whose influence was paramount, even in the parishes not favoured with the Gospel.

Who, then, and what were "the men"? A fair answer to this question is all the defence they require, for theirs is a character that can only suffer by being hid.

When a godly Highland minister discerned a promise of usefulness in a man who seemed to have been truly converted unto God, he brought him gradually forward into a more public position, by calling him first to pray, and then "to speak to the question," at the ordinary congregational meetings. According to the manner in which he approved himself there was the prospect of his being enrolled among "the Friday speakers" on communion occasions. It was thus the order of "the men" was established, and thus the body of "the men" was formed.

The only peculiarity about them, besides their godliness, was their service in the fellowship meeting. This has, to some eyes, the wild look of a great irregularity. It is thought that "the men" were pushed forward into the position of public speakers by the current of popular feeling, and that the ministers were compelled to share with them their own place in order to reserve any part of it to themselves. Than this there cannot be a greater mistake. The peculiar service of "the men" was not thrust upon those ministers who were what ministers should be. By such it was freely and deliberately adopted, and none of them had ever cause to regret that it was. "The men" were never found to be enemies to due ecclesiastical order, though they failed in learning to submit to undue ecclesiastical tyranny. They were influenced by no feeling of disrespect to the office of the ministry, nor were they disposed to take a place in the house of the Lord not given them by the Lord of the house. It was not in their heart, it is true, to esteem the individuals who found it their interest to hold, while it was their practice to degrade, the office of the ministry; but it is only in their respect for the office itself that the true reason of this can be found. Valuable was the help and cheering the encouragement which a godly minister always received from their prayers, their counsels, and their labours.

The great object of the fellowship meeting was the mutual comfort and edification of believers with a special reference to the cases of such as were exercised with fears as to their interest in Christ. And how was it conducted? At first only communicants were present; but, latterly, admission became indiscriminate. The minister presides, and, after prayer, praise, and the reading of a portion of Scripture, he calls on any one who is anxious to propose a question to the meeting, to do so. This call is responded to by some man who rises, mentions a passage of Scripture describing some feature of the Christian character, and expresses his desire to ascertain the marks of those whom the passage describes, and the various respects in which they may differ from merely nominal Christians. The scope of the passage of Scripture is then opened up by the minister, and the exact import of the question founded upon it is explained. He then calls by name, successively, on such as are of repute for piety, experience, and gifts to ''speak to the question.'' One after another rises, as he is called, states briefly his view of the question, and, without attempting either to expound Scripture, or to deliver an exhortation, or venturing to parade his own experience, speaks from the heart what he has felt, and feared, and enjoyed under the power of the truth. Thereafter the minister sums up all that has been said, correcting, confirming, and expanding, as may be necessary, and makes a practical improvement of the whole. The person who proposed the question is then usually called to engage in prayer, and, with praise and the benediction, the meeting is closed. Such was the fellowship meeting in the good days of the Fathers in Ross-shire.

''The men'' seem, to some, to have been taken out of their proper place when called to address a congregation, and to have assumed work properly and exclusively the minister's. They must be quite ignorant of ''the men'' and of their work with whom this objection can have any weight. If they were accustomed to expound, or if they attempted to preach, it might be said that they were stepping out of their proper place and invading the province of the minister; but they who were worthy of a place among "the men" never attempted to do so. They but spake to one another of their mutual fears and trials, hopes and joys; and the position, as office-bearers, held by the most of them, and the gifts which the Lord had conferred on them all, entitled them to do so in the more public position of the fellowship meeting. Never was a godly minsiter's office less endangered than when he was countenancing and directing their service in "speaking to the question," and often has the time thus spent by him been to his own soul a season of refreshing.

There are many who think that uneducated persons, such as "the men," could not possibly deliver addresses that might edify their hearers. Those who required "the excellency of speech and of wisdom" in order to be pleased, would certainly not be gratified at the fellowship meeting, but those who "desired the sincere milk of the word that" they "might grow thereby," would as certainly be profited. Of such learning as makes one proud, "the men" had none; but they knew their Bibles as few besides have known them. Their clear views of the Gospel system might bring a blush on the face of some Professors of divinity if they heard and understood them; and some Doctors, however learned, might sit at their feet as they spake of the sorrows and the joys of the Christian's life. Some of them were men of distinguished talent, and all their mental vigour, untrammeled by learning, they brought to bear upon the things of God. Never, surely, is there a more attractive exercise of intellect than when, divested of all literary acquirement, it enters directly into "the mysteries of the kingdom," and comes forth in a panoply of Scripture truth. Light from heaven then irradiates all the gifts of the speaker. Traces of learning, mingled with the halo of this light, would be spots of darkness. Some of "the men" were able speakers. Orators they were, without attempting to be so, and utterly unconscious of their gift, who could powerfully affect the feelings of their hearers. Some of them gave utterance to sayings that could not be forgotten, and a few of which would earn a fame for genius in a more public sphere.

Of the question, "How far lay agency may be employed for the edification of the Church," the wisest practical solution has been furnished in the service of the fellowship meeting. It is surely desirable that, if there are talented and godly men in a congregation, an opportunity should be afforded for securing to others the benefit of these gifts with which the Lord has endowed them. If He has made them "apt to teach," an opportunity to teach should be given them by the Church. This should be provided, so as not to invade the province of the ordained teacher, and so as to conserve and support the authority of his office. By no summary process ought a man to be converted into a preacher, however shining his gifts, and however eminent his godliness. But is he therefore to be kept silent? May no opportunity be given to him to exhort his brethren, publicly as well as privately, so as to secure to the Church at large the benefit of his stores of Christian knowledge and experience? All these conditions have been met in the service of the fellowship meeting. There an opportunity to exercise their gifts for the good of the Church, and without the least prejudice to the position and influence of the minister, was given to such as the Lord had qualified. How strange it is that some who neglect to avail themselves of such an arrangement, and who are disposed to frown upon it where it has been adopted, should not hesitate to exalt into the position even of evangelists, neophytes, with crude views of the doctrines of the Gospel, owning subjection to no ecclesiastical authority, and furnishing no security whatever for the prudence and the purity of their doctrine and their life!

The service in which "the men" were employed was useful as a test. In the good days of the Fathers the discernment of the Church was keen, and very rarely could a man who was a stranger to a life of godliness be approved at the fellowship meeting. Satan required to do his utmost in making a passable hypocrite in those days. He sometimes, even then, succeeded in foisting a counterfeit on the confidence of the Church, but it was not often that he tried it. Usually, "of the rest durst no man join himself to them." Through this ordeal the eldership had to pass ere they found a place in a Session over which a man of God presided. It would be well if this kind of trial were universal. The application of such a test might, in some cases, allow no Session at all; but it may be fairly questioned whether this is a valid objection to its use. Now, and in some places, let a man's religion be all on the outside of him, if it is only a decent garb to look at from a distance, and if he is a man of influence, or of money, or of talent, this is quite enough to win for him an elder's place. An uneducated but godly and praying elder would be better than a host of such men as he; but, better still the man in whom the gifts and the influence of the one were sanctified by the grace given to the other.

It is partly true that "the men" were peculiar in their dress, but it is not all true that they adopted any kind of badge, or that they wore a uniform that distinguished them as a class. In the circle in which they moved there were attempts made by the careless and worldly to follow, at a distance, the mutations of fashion in their attire. "The men" would not, and merely on that account their dress was peculiar. It was often the case that they wore long hair, partly because a regard to appearances did not remind them of cutting it, and partly that they might discountenance the attempts at clipping and combing "after the fashion" by which many around them evidenced their conformity to the world. It is true, also, that they often appeared with a handkerchief on their heads, but so did many besides them, who met to worship under a scorching sun, and regarded it as unbecoming to have a hat or bonnet on their heads. If their dress seemed peculiar, it was only because it was old-fashioned, even in the Highlands. Its singularity was not owing to any affectation, or to an undue regard to what was external and trivial.

Of the orthodoxy of "the men" of Ross-shire no defence is required; on the ground of alleged unsoundness in the faith none of all their enemies ever ventured to bring a charge against them. A strong aversion to any deviation from the authorised standards of doctrine characterised them as a class, and often have the ministers who ventured to challenge their views been forced to feel, in an encounter with them, how little, as compared with "the men," they themselves knew of their Bibles, or had studied the standards which, to win stipends, they subscribed. A few of them once were present when a sermon was preached giving a faulty exposition of the text, and containing an infusion of Arminianism. On the next day there was a fellowship meeting, at which the minister who preached that sermon presided. According to a preconcerted plan, the text of the Sabbath sermon was proposed as the passage on which the question should be founded at the meeting. The minister demurred, but could not succeed in getting the question replaced by another. One man after another spoke exposing the unsoundness of the doctrine delivered from the pulpit. The result was that the preacher betook himself in self-defence to the Bible and to the "Confession of Faith," but the weapons which he found in that armoury, instead of being used by himself in beating down "the men," were employed by the Spirit of the Lord in overturning his own views, in slaying his former hopes, and in laying low his soul at the footstool of mercy. From that day this minister never preached as he had preached before.

It is due to their memory to add that they "adorned the doctrine of God their Saviour in all things." By the purity of their lives, they constrained all who observed them to regard them as Christians. Their enemies did call them "bigots," "enthusiasts," and "fanatics," but they did not dare to say they were not Christians. They were compelled to acknowledge that they were "sincere," "upright," and "well-meaning," though "very straitlaced" and "righteous overmuch."

And they loved one another. Their position being one of greater eminence than that of mere "private Christians," and opportunities of sowing discord among them being all the more manifold because of the peculiar service in which they were employed, it is quite marvellous how few instances of unseemly quarrels their enemies can record against them. Sometimes differences would arise, but they were felt by them all as a family affliction would be felt. In such cases, a peace-maker would always be found. Sometimes his task would be made an easy one. One of them, hearing of a quarrel between two of his brethren, set off at once to make peace. Meeting one of the offenders, he asked, "Is it true that you and James have quarrelled?" "Oh, yes; alas! it is quite true," was the reply; "but

James is not to be blamed — the fault is all mine." "If I find James," he remarked, "in the same state of mind, I expect very soon to see you at one again." On reaching the other, he said. "I am sorry to hear that you have quarrelled with John." "Oh yes," he replied, "but it was my hasty temper that did all the mischief." "Come with me, then," the peacemaker said, "and confess your fault to your brother." He at once agreed to accompany him; and, no sooner did the separated brethren meet, than they embraced each other, mutually forgave and were forgiven, and continued ever after "in the bond of peace."

Two of them, happening to differ about the proper interpretation of a passage of Scripture, lost temper, and as, alas! too often happens, quarrelled over the Bible. For some time thereafter they would not speak to each other. Some of their brethren interfered, but they found them implacable. At last it was agreed to refer the matter to the arbitration of Hugh Ross of Kilmuir and Hugh Buie. A meeting took place, at which the two who had quarrelled and the two arbiters were only present. After engaging in prayer, one of the Hughs said to the other, "Brother, we must be on our guard against being led into adopting instead of settling the quarrel of these men"; and in token of their love, and to seal their resolution still to love, they embraced each other. The sight of these two godly men locked in each other's arms quite overcame the disputants, who were looking on. The thought arose simultaneously in the mind of each of them, "These are true Christians, for they love one another, and if we were like them we would not have quarrelled." Looking at one another, they could not refrain from following the example which was given them; they rushed to a mutual embrace, all strife was at an end; and their hearts once more united, they found it easy to "see eye to eye." The arbiters succeeded, by the example of their love, in securing a result which they would have failed to achieve by all their tact and influence.

The earliest traditions of "the men" are clustered around the name of John Munro, the celebrated caird of Kiltearn.[1] An interesting

[1] In 1568 the Reader at Kilterne was Angus Neilson, and in 1574 Farquhar

account of his conversion is given in the memoir of Mr Hogg, to which the reader is referred. One anecdote of him only will be given here.

The case of a pious man in the parish of Logie-Easter having been pressed upon his spirit, his anxiety about him became so great that he could not refrain from going to visit him. On a stormy winter day he started on his journey, and with considerable difficulty reached the house of his friend. No sooner had they saluted than his friend threw himself on a seat, and burst into tears. "This is not the welcome I expected," John said; "I had hoped you would have been glad to see me." "What grieves me," was the reply, "is that, after you have come so far on such a stormy day, I have no food that I can set before you." "I know now why I have come," the caird said, and throwing on the table a piece of bread which he had carried in his pocket, he hurried out of the house. Setting his face on the west again, not a house by the way in which he knew there was a friend to the poor did he pass on his journey back to Kiltearn without entering it, and telling of the poverty of his friend, urging them all at once to send him a supply of food. In the morning of the morrow, horses, laden with creels full of provisions, began to arrive at the empty house in Arbol, and before that day closed a supply of meal, and butter, and cheese was stored up in it that sufficed for "a year and a day."

Before the death of John Munro the famous Alexander Ross,

Monro. — *Orig. Paroch.*

Donald Munro, descended from the family of Coul, is said by Dr Harry Robertson to have been parson here (the Protestant minister). His appointment as Commissioner was renewed in August, 1573; his commission was to plant kirks within the bounds of Ross, given by the Assembly, 26th June, 1563. Tradition says he lived in Castle Craig, crossed the Firth by boats, and preached on the Lord's Days. — *Fasti.*

The *Caird* was a crofter who had his residence a mile to the west of the modern village, Evanton, in the hollow to the south of the farm, Cnockancuirn. True religion prevailed among his descendants in every generation of them. Devoted ministers of the Gospel arose among them, such as the celebrated Rev. Mr Munro of Halkirk and Rev. Christopher Munro of Strathy. His offspring are still here and there among the people of the parishes on the north side of the Cromarty Firth, and in them are found persons who are of the salt of the earth. — *Editor.*

better known as Alister Og, the godly weaver of Edderton,[1] was born, and perhaps "born again." He just outlived the first quarter of the eighteenth century, but, as he was an old man when he died, the greater part of his life must have been passed in the century before.

Even in his day there were favoured spots in Ross-shire that were beginning to be as the garden of the Lord,[2] and his great eminence was not owing to his being a solitary witness for God. There was then in Edderton a minister by whose doctrine even Alister could be fed, and there was a lady of Balnagown who deemed it an honour to have the godly weaver as her guest. Anxious enquirers, too, from surrounding districts used to visit him for advice.

On one occasion there came a pious man to consult him about the meaning of the counsel, "Pray without ceasing." On his arrival he

[1] The Abbey of Fearn, founded early in the 13th century, by Farquhard, Earl of Ross, "beside Kincardin, in Strathcarrin," stood at Fearn, probably Middle Fearn, in this parish, where the convent appears to have remained for about fifteen years before its removal to New Fearn, and where vestiges of its buildings seem to have been visible till the end of the 16th century. In the year 1574 the Reader at Eddirtayn had for his stipend twenty marks and the kirk lands. The parish was supplied by Donald Symsoun, Reader, from 1576 to 1583. He was presented to the vicarage by James VI, 26th October, 1583. — *Origin, Paroch, and Scott's Fasti.*

Alister Og's minister seems to have been Hector Fraser, who was translated from Kincardine; admitted to Edderton on the 4th May, 1709; died 17th May, 1729, in the 31st year of his ministry.

If not the above, it was Robert Robertson, who was translated from Loth, and admitted 29th July, 1730; died, 13th December, 1740, aged about 50, in the 20th year of his ministry. — *Scott's Fasti.*

[2] A wave of spiritual blessing passed over the parishes bordering on the Cromarty Firth in the generation that arose after Prelacy. The Presbyterian ministers who succeeded the "curates" were godly men, devoted in a marked way to their Master's service, and of unwearied diligence in instructing the people. At the Revolution in some parishes of Ross-shire many of the people were not far in advance of barbarism. As the "curates," who turned Presbyterian to keep their places, were removed from the world, their parishes were supplied by men of prayer, who were not satisfied with a mere round of duties, but laboured to win souls, and they were not disappointed. The reader is referred to that most interesting book, "Revivals of the 18th Century." — *Editor.*

found Alister busy digging his croft. "You are well employed, Alister," he said on coming up to him. "If delving and praying, praying and delving, be good employment, I am," was the answer, which met the enquirer's difficulty before he had stated it.

Once, late at night, a stranger applied at Alister's door for a night's lodging. His wife was unwilling to admit him, but Alister, "not forgetful to entertain strangers," at once invited him to come in, and gave him the best his house could afford. On rising next morning the wife found that the stranger had gone, and had carried off a web which her husband had just finished to order. "Didn't I tell you," she said, after hurrying to Alister with the tidings of the theft, "not to admit that man; you yourself will now be suspected of doing away with the web, and what will become of us?" "I admitted the stranger," was her husband's reply, "because the Lord commanded me; and if there is no other way of defending His cause, He will send the man who stole the web back with it again." That day was very misty, and the thief spent it wearily wandering, with the web on his back, over the Hill of Edderton. After nightfall, as Alister and his wife were sitting by the ingle, they heard a knock at the door, on opening which, whom should they see on the threshold but their guest of the night before. He had wandered, not knowing whither, till his eye was arrested and his course directed by the light that twinkled in Alister's window; and now, much to his surprise and confusion, he finds himself throwing the web off his back in the house from which he had stolen it.

Alister had once a sore battle with self — a giant who has been found by all who ever encountered him to have "seven lives, seven guises, and seven hands." Nothing would satisfy his enemy but to wrest from poor Alister his all of experience, service, and suffering, leaving nothing with him for Him who had bought him with His blood, and to whose service he was sworn. The conflict was severe, and Alister, though he would not yield, found his strength to be but weakness and his wisdom but folly in the fight. He resolved, therefore, to call for help from above, and he devoted a day to fasting, heart-searching, and prayer on the summit of the Hill of Edderton. The Lord came to his help, and Alister was delivered from the grasp of his enemy, and he gave himself without reserve anew unto the Lord. In the flush of victory he began to descend the hill, and on coming near his house, and observing his neighbours closing a busy day's work on their crofts, the thought at once sprang up in his mind, "how very much better I have been employed to-day than these." Telling the story himself afterwards, and referring to this suggestion, he added, "The fellow I thought I had left stark dead on the top of the Hill of Edderton, I found as lively as ever in my heart."

As he was standing one morning in front of his house, his wife, looking out through the window, observed him smiling with joy. Anxious to know what amused him, she came out to inquire. Pointing to his cow, which lay dead before the door, he said, "I was rejoicing because mine was a God that could not die like yours."

His minister, in one of his sermons, pressed strongly upon Christians the duty of seeking and the profit of attaining "an assurance of God's love." Alister was deeply affected by that sermon; and, instead of returning to his house on that evening, he repaired to his usual haunt on the hill. There he remained all that night, and a day and a night besides, pleading with the Lord and examining himself till he attained the assurance which he sought. On Tuesday he descended from the hill, and went straight to the manse. Meeting the minister, he at once asked him, "Did you preach your last sermon according to your own experience?" The minister was able to assure him that he had. Alister then solemnly said, "Not many sermons more will you ever preach." And so it happened; for in a very short time the minister died, and not long after Alister followed him to the "Father's house."

Hugh Ross of Kilmuir represents the generation of "the men" that succeeded Alister Og and his contemporaries. He was a man of considerable mental vigour, of singular godliness, of an unblemished life, favoured with great nearness to God, and with a manifest blessing resting on his labours. During the years of his ignorance, he was known as a powerful, handsome youth, glorying in his symmetry and strength, the leader at the shinty matches, and the best dancer in the district. Getting a new Highland dress, which he thought very fine, and which he was anxious to display, he went, on the Saturday of a communion season at Fearn, to show it off before the congregation. Choosing the most conspicuous seat, there he showed himself in his pride before the eyes of all. Mr Porteous preached on that day, and before the sermon was over an arrow, "shot at a venture," had found a joint in the proud youth's harness, and pierced him to the heart. Deep were his convictions thereafter, and for months he walked under the shadow of death. Each Sabbath now found Hugh at church, but across its threshold he would not venture to pass. He stood alone and desolate outside each time he came, the drops from the eaves often falling on his head, and sometimes, in winter, congealing into clusters of icicles from his hair. But what affected merely his body he felt not. He was listening to the Word of God, with an immortal soul at stake, as if each sermon he heard was to decide its destiny for ever. One of the elders, an aged and godly man, felt the warmest interest in the stricken and desolate youth; and on a Sabbath of snow and drift, as Hugh was standing outside as usual, he crept up towards him, pushed him across the threshold, and shut him in. But his time of deliverance had now come, and in proportion to his former bondage was the thoroughness of his liberty, and to his former distress the intensity of his joy. He became "a burning and a shining light," was chosen catechist of Kilmuir, and was highly honoured and blessed in his work. Three of the children of the old elder were brought to Christ under his instructions, and he thus received from the Lord a most precious reward for his kindness to Hugh in the day of his distress. It is said that, on one occasion, no fewer than seven, and on another, twelve persons were awakened under his teaching, who were afterwards approved followers of the Lamb.

Perhaps of all "the men" of Ross-shire, the most famous was Hugh Ross, commonly called Hugh Buie. It was in Alness he resided, when, before his twentieth year, he first "knew the grace of God in truth." He removed afterwards to Rosskeen, and his last days were spent in Resolis.

Mr James Fraser of Alness was his father in Christ. After the death of that eminent minister, a preacher was presented to the parish of Alness whom Hugh opposed with all his influence. This man having been thrust into the charge, Hugh was greatly distressed, and was so violently excited that, being naturally keen tempered, it was easy for the Tempter to persuade him that all his agitation was but the sinful fretting of his temper, and that there was no exercise of grace at all in the ferment of his spirit. On the first Sabbath after the induction, he resolved to go to hear Mr Porteous. But a parish intervened between him and Kilmuir, and if he went by the usual road he would meet the people as they were assembling to the church of Rosskeen. So he determined to walk along the sea-shore, that he might reach Kilmuir unobserved. This was then comparatively easy, as the villages now built along the shore were not then in existence. Mr Porteous preached that day on "the hidden man of the heart" (1 Peter 3: 4). To illustrate his subject, he referred to the ark and its coverings in the wilderness. "Its outside covering was made of badgers' skins," he said, "and the fur of this animal always points against the wind, and as one looked on it, rough and ruffled, as a breeze was blowing on the tabernacle, it seemed very unlikely that under it the precious ark was hidden. Thus is 'the hidden man of the heart' often hidden under a fretful temper; and there is one now present who has lately felt his mind so ruffled under a trying providence that he finds it impossible to believe that 'the ornament of a meek and quiet spirit' can be his at all. But let us raise this covering and examine what is under it''; and then removing one covering after another, he conducted Hugh at last to "the hidden man of the heart" within himself, and the Holy Spirit sealed to his soul, by the truth, a satisfying evidence of grace. Cheered by this seasonable comfort, he returned home by the public road, declaring, after his return, that he was now ready to go to Kilmuir in the face of all difficulties and under the eyes of all observers.

Over eighty years his Christian course on earth extended, and during all that time he continued to "adorn the doctrine of God." He was unable to read even his Bible, but he knew it well, and believed, loved, and lived its precious truths. But, though quite uneducated, he was a man of rare talent. As a speaker he was peculiarly clear and concise. In a few terse and vigorous expressions, fraught with thought and seasoned with grace, he conveyed more instruction than could be derived from many a learned and laboured treatise on the subject on which he spoke.

He was always slow to rise when called upon to speak. Having on one occasion to go with some cattle to a remote place on the hills of Lochbroom, he was obliged to remain all night in the house of the farmer to whose care they were consigned. His host never bent his knee before his household, and without doing so on that night he offered to conduct Hugh to his bed. His guest at once refused to go till they had read the Word of God together and joined in prayer. The farmer agreed to allow family worship if Hugh himself would conduct it, but, according to his usual custom, he declined, and urged the farmer himself to do it. The latter at last consented, but such was his prayer that Hugh was quite shocked and sickened before it was over, and sorely repented of his refusal. He slept none on going to bed, and starting at the dawn of next morning he reached the house of Hector Holm in the evening. Remaining there all night he was present at family worship. After the reading of the chapter, Hector asked his friend to pray, and, expecting the usual delay, he set himself slowly to close the Bible and to fold his spectacles. But, to his surprise, scarcely was the request uttered when Hugh was on his knees and the prayer begun. So soon as it was over his host asked him to account for the change that had come over him since he saw him last. Hugh then told the story of the night before. Dr Macdonald, hearing the story, would ever afterwards say to him when he did not rise at once on being called— "I find we must send you again to Clascarnich."

Removing in his last days to Resolis, he sat under the ministry of Mr Sage. Seated in his usual place in church on his last Sabbath, which proved to be his last day on earth, he seemed unusually happy, his countenance radiant with the light of the joy of his heart as his soul was feeding on "the bread of life." After sermon he accompanied the minister to the manse. Having sat at the dinner-table, he asked a blessing in his own clear unctuous way, and having taken up his spoon he quietly laid it down again, leant back on his chair, and, without a moan or a struggle, fell "asleep in Jesus" in the ninety-ninth year of his age.

Seldom has a lovelier Christian character been developed than that of Donald Mitchell, the celebrated catechist of Kilmuir. Amiable in disposition, vigorous in intellect, knowing in early youth "the grace of God in truth," and trained under a powerful Gospel ministry, he entered on his public career as a witness for God with an equipment for his work to which but few attain. As a speaker he was peculiarly solemn, clear, and pathetic. His words came carefully weighed from his well-balanced mind, while coming fervent with love from his broken heart. At the fellowship meeting he has often carried "a word in season" to a weary soul. As a catechist he was quite unrivalled. Hector Holm used to say of him that "as a Friday speaker he had his ups and downs like other men, but that as a catechist he was always excellent." Patient when he met with ignorance or error, discriminating accurately between the various dispositions with which he had to deal, clear and pointed in examination and skilful in bringing the truth by the right course to the conscience, he is generally regarded as the model catechist of Ross-shire. No greater boon could be conferred on a godly minister than the aid of such a man as the godly and judicious Donald Mitchell.

John Clark, Cromarty, may be claimed as one of "the men" of Ross-shire, for it was there he usually heard the Gospel, and there alone he had stated opportunities of taking part in the fellowship meetings. He was a noble-looking man. When his tall figure became erect as he rose up to speak, and when with both his hands he threw back his white flowing locks, exposing his expressive face, he looked a man that might have graced a senate. As a speaker he was deliberate, clear, and persuasive. Never tedious and never trifling, he arrested and sustained the solemn attention of his hearers.

There was a young man in Resolis who was subject to dreadful fits of epilepsy. His father bethought him of bringing a few praying Christians together to plead with God for the recovery of his son. Before doing so he consulted his minister, who, after ascertaining that he was influenced by no superstitious feeling, and actuated by no improper motives, allowed him to carry out his project. John Clark and two others were invited to meet, and agreed to the distressed father's proposal. John was the first who engaged in prayer when they met, and it pleased the Lord to grant him such nearness to Himself, and such encouragement to ask what there was no general warrant to seek, that ere his prayer was concluded he expressed his assurance that his petition would be granted. And so it was, for the young man was never afterwards attacked as he had so often been before.

He once caused no small commotion at Cromarty by declaring very emphatically at a fellowship meeting that not a builder or tailor in Cromarty could be saved. All the masons and needlemen were vastly indignant, not understanding that John referred to "the builders" who rejected the "chief stone of the corner," and to all who were patching with rags a righteousness for themselves.

There is one who, stretching his memory across more than thirty years, to the days of his boyhood, can recollect a part of one of John's addresses at a fellowship meeting. The homeliness of the illustration drew the attention of the boy, and, falling into the mistake of the Cromarty tradesmen, he was ready to cry at the prospect held out, as he thought, to himself, and to be angry at the prophet of evil. "I don't pity you," he said, "while, yet a child in your father's house, your mother places your food at stated times before you, and you know not the pain of anxiety, the pinching of want, nor the drudgery of labour. But wait a little and these pleasant days will be gone, and you will have then to set out to your daily toil in the morning with your mattock on your shoulder and a barley-cake in your pocket as your 'daily bread.'" The use of this illustration the reader is left to determine for himself; but it has afforded no unprofitable matter for reflection to him who first heard it as a boy.

Several members of his family having emigrated to America, he, in his old age, resolved to follow them, much to the surprise of all who knew him, and to the sorrow of all who loved him. He reached the land of his adoption, shone there as a light amid the darkness for a few years, but pined till he died amid the memories of the land of his birth. His body now lies in the soil of America, and his spirit is resting in its mansion in glory.

Roderick Mackenzie, better known by the name of Rory Phadrig, was a man of sterling worth. With a horror of affectation that made him afraid to show in his manner the warmth of his heart, a stranger would have thought him to be an impersonation of rudeness. "I'm but a rude crabbed bodach," he used to say of himself, and to those whose religion he suspected, he never tried to be otherwise. His manner as a speaker was quite peculiar. He had a voice that could not be tamed into melody, and he was not the man to make an effort to subdue it. It was not loud, but deep-toned and harsh. He was never tedious when he spoke, and what he said was always to the point. He would omit no opportunity of warning the hypocrite, and of commending to the Christian watchfulness and prayer. The carnal mind was always referred to in a way that indicated the deadly war that was ever waged between it and Rory; and he always reserved his harshest tones for expressing his feelings in reference to its workings. In prayer or in address he soon came to the cross, and fresh and unctuous were all his utterances regarding the love of Jesus.

There were three classes of professors in whom it was very difficult for Rory to see any good; those who, elated with spiritual pride, became disaffected to the stated ministry of the gospel; the affected sentimentalists, who made a parade of their feelings; and those who might be suspected of having all their religion in their heads.

It was under the preaching of Mr Macadam, during his ministry in Cromarty, that Rory was first brought to a knowledge of the truth. Not long thereafter he removed to Strathconon, where he was at a great distance from the ministers whom he most loved to hear. "Beware," he once said at a "Friday meeting," "that you don't make idols of your ministers; it was this that banished me to the bleak hills of Strathconon."

He frequently went to Lochcarron to visit and to hear Mr Lachlan. By that eminent minister he was greatly beloved, and many an hour of sweet and profitable converse have they spent together. The only time Rory ever succeeded in infusing music into his voice was when repeating, as he often did in an ecstasy of spiritual enjoyment, Mr Lachlan's poem on Redemption; and his only attempt at poetry was composing an elegy in verse in his praise. To the minister of Killearnan he was devotedly attached, and his love was fully returned. Few of the cares and sorrows of either were unshared by the other. In his distant Highland glen Rory would know when Mr Kennedy was in distress; and when he came to Killearnan all his own fears and sorrows were told to him from the pulpit. "I had just two days of heaven on earth," he once said, "when Mr Lachlan preached on the Babe in Bethlehem, and Mr Kennedy on the Covenant of Grace. The one helped me to find the child Jesus in the vile stable within me, and the other helped me to read the name of Rory Phadrig in the list of the chosen, for whom Christ became surety in the Covenant."

Throughout his Christian course, he was much given to prayer, watchful in his conduct, industrious in his calling, wide and warm in his sympathies. During the last few years of his life he was employed as catechist in the Parish of Urray, and so acquitted himself in his work as to disappoint all the fears and to exceed all the hopes of those who appreciated and loved him. It was his mellowed old age he gave to his work; and while retaining still the peculiarities of his manner, he mingled his faithfulness with much affectionate tenderness. Death found him on his knees, on the scene, and in the midst of his last labours of love.

Were there no reason to believe that one more qualified for the work will undertake a minuter description of the men, and a more comprehensive record of their sayings, the sample now given would have been greatly enlarged. The time was when, in a single parish, twenty could have been found any one of whom would, in our day, be ranked amongst "the first three" whom the whole county can produce. "The King's mowing" has long since taken away the rich produce of the best days of Ross-shire. "The latter growth" is rapidly disappearing; and desolate will be its spiritual aspect, and dismal the prospect of its future, if "the men" shall be utterly removed from the north. Verily it is high time to cry "By whom shall Jacob arise? For he is small."

CHAPTER IV

THE RELIGION OF ROSS-SHIRE

THE ministry, of which a description was attempted, could not fail to leave a deep impression, of its own peculiar character, on the views, feelings, and habits of the people. The power of the pulpit was paramount in Ross-shire, and the people became, to a great extent, plastic to its influence. The preachers could mould the opinions and habits of their hearers, without any counteracting influences, besides such as invariably operate, to distort the impression which they desired to produce. In such circumstances, these men of God failed not to realise their own ideal, to a great extent, in the effects of their ministry. But the attained result was of the Lord; and the fabric reared by these ''wise master builders'' bears the traces of their skill no further than it proves that they were ''labourers together with God.'' It was not a monument to themselves these devoted men were building but a house for God; and in its ''form and fashion'' we have abundant proof that in raising it they kept their eye on the ''pattern'' given them by the Lord.

And what was the result of their ministry? In order to ascertain this we look back on one of the congregations of Ross-shire in its best days.

A gifted man of God is the minister. A goodly number of his hearers have been truly converted unto God, by whom he is loved, encouraged, and aided. By the unconverted the authority of his office is respected, although their feeling towards their pastor may have in it as much of fear as of love. A catechist, a godly, wise, and gifted man, is employed in teaching the people from house to house. The session is formed of elders, each one of whom is a man of prayer and of a well-established reputation for godliness, and all of whom command the respect and submission of the people. *Such was a Ross-shire congregation in the good days of the Fathers.*

On Sabbath they all meet in the house of God. The Lord Himself is in the midst of them; the Word is rightly divided; hungry souls are fed with "the finest of the wheat"; some of "the whole" are wounded; and some of the wounded ones are healed. The public service over, the people return to their homes, and by the way they form into companies around some of the Lord's people, who are speaking of the sermon, and bringing again before themselves and others the precious lessons which it furnished. In the evening, district meetings are held, each presided over by an elder, or by some man of repute for godliness. After prayer and praise and the reading of a portion of Scripture, a certain number of the questions of the Shorter Catechism are asked and answered, and notes of the sermons heard during the day are repeated. Time is allowed for family duties, and in many a household the incense of prayer and praise ascends from the family altar to God. *Such was an ordinary Ross-shire Sabbath in the good days of the Fathers.*

Fortnightly, on Monday at noon, there is alternately a prayer and a fellowship meeting, after which a meeting of session is generally held. On Tuesday and Wednesday, during winter and spring, the minister "holds diets of catechising." The residents in a certain district are gathered into one place — the church, a school, or a barn — and after praise, prayer, and an exposition of one of the questions of the Shorter Catechism in course, each person, from the district for the day, is minutely and searchingly examined. All attend and all are catechised. Each individual conscience is thus reached by the truth, the exact amount of knowledge possessd by each of his hearers, as well as his state of feeling, ascertained by the minister, a clear knowledge of the fundamental doctrines of the gospel communicated, and valuable materials gathered for the work of the pulpit. During the remaining days of the week the minister's work is in secret, except when a call to visit comes to him, in which he hears the voice of his Master. On four evenings of the week the catechist is employed in his peculiar work. He goes over the several districts of the parish as the pastor's pioneer, and his diets of

catechising are conducted almost quite like those of the minister.
All the people attend to be examined by him, and often have his
instructions been signally blessed. On a set evening of each week
prayer-meetings are conducted by the elders in the several districts,
and such men found in those days congenial employment in frequent
converse with inquirers. *Such was the ordinary weekly work in one
of the Ross-shire congregations in the good days of the Fathers.*

A Communion season is approaching. It has been timeously
announced, that it may be known "far and wide," and that the
praying people may be bearing it on their spirits before the throne of
grace. The minister preaches a suitable course of sermons on several
preceding Sabbaths. The Lord's people are stirred up to seek a
special manifestation of His power and glory. A few who propose to
seek admission to the Lord's Table are deeply exercised about the
solemn step they contemplate, and faithfully and tenderly are they
dealt with by both ministers and elders. As the appointed time
draws nigh, special meetings for prayer are held, and, with holy
solicitude, all the preparatory arrangements are made. The *Fast-Day*
is come. Eminent ministers have arrived to take part in the solemn
services. Many of the Lord's people are gathering. From as many as
forty parishes they come; but lodgings they will easily procure, as
the parish people are striving for the pleasure of entertaining them.
Suitable discourses are preached in Gaelic in the open field, and to a
small English congregation in the church, and in the evening
prayer-meetings are held in the various districts of the parish. On
Friday, the day of self-examination, the only public service is in the
open air. A large crowd is gathered. "In the tent" there are several
godly ministers. The service is that of a fellowship meeting, such as
has already been described, but now with special reference to the
solemn duties of a Communion Sabbath. There are two questions
proposed successively to secure variety. Strangers only are called to
speak, and even of these only "the flower," for there are so many.
Not fewer than thirty will have spoken before the service is over.
Blessed indeed to many souls have these "Friday meetings" been.
The services on *Saturday*, the day of preparation, are conducted as
on Thursday, but, owing to the gathering influx of strangers, the

congregation outside is greatly larger than on the Fast-Day. At the
close of the service tokens are distributed. Prayer meetings are held
throughout the parish in the evening; and while the ministers are
preparing for the solemn work of the Sabbath, many are the
petitions that ascend in their behalf to Him who hath "the treasure"
to dispense, and of whom is "the excellency of the power." In
many instances, these prayer meetings have been protracted all
night. So sensible were the people of the presence of the Lord that
they could not forsake the place where they enjoyed it; and they
found "the joy of the Lord" a sweet substitute for sleep. On
Sabbath, the day of Communion, an immense crowd is gathered
before the tent. As many as eight thousand are there. The "Beauty
of the Lord" is on the assembly of His people; and before the
service is over, many a soul has had reason to say, "It is good to be
here." On *Monday*, the day of thanksgiving, a crowd almost as
large as that on Sabbath is assembled; and often has "the last"
been found to be the "great day of the feast." The closing service of
the Communion season is now over, and then comes the solemn
parting! How affecting do the Lord's servants and people feel the
scene before them to be, as that multitude disperses, never to meet
all together again till the vast congregation of the "last day" has
assembled! What touching farewells are now exchanged between the
Christians who enjoyed with each other, and together with the
Lord, such sweet communion since they met a few days before!
There are few tearless eyes, but the weeping is expressive of
gratitude as surely as of sorrow. *Such was a Communion season in
the good days of the Fathers in Ross-shire.*

All this was true of Ross-shire in its best days; but only then, and
even then only in those parishes that enjoyed a spiritual ministry.
At the same time, the influence of the Gospel spread over the
community. It reached the parishes in which there was no evangelical
ministry, not only in individual cases of conversion, but so as to win
the esteem of the whole body of the people. This was owing to the
commanding position their godliness and their gifts acquired for the
pious ministers of those days, and to the unblemished lives of the
Christians who were edified by their preaching. Both ministers and

private Christians in those days were such that "the people magnified them."

There are not awanting some who suspect the healthfulness of the religious spirit which was thus so extensively excited. As there are certain peculiarities which distinguish it from the type assumed by the religious feeling in the Lowlands, the Southrons have been anxious to make out that the difference is owing to some defect or excess that may be charged against the north. The Ross-shire preaching, they say, was too experimental, and in the religion of those who were trained under it, there was, in consequence, a faulty excess of subjectiveness. To the radical peculiarity thus indicated, whether it be accounted a defect or an advantage, may be traced all the developments of the religious spirit in the Highlands that form its distinctive character, as compared with the Christianity of the Lowlands.

Those who think the comparison unfavourable to the pious Highlander, regard him as prone to attach undue importance to mere "frames and feelings," having never learned to distinguish between the foundation and the building — the work of Christ for him, and the work of the Spirit wihin him. He is suspected of having a fictitious standard of experience, which, like a Procrustes' bed, he uses as a means of torture to himself, and as an unrelenting test of the Christianity of others. A Highland Christian is, therefore, in their esteem, a gloomy bigot, as compared with the more cheerful and liberal Christians of the south. To the same source they would trace the want of that activity which distinguishes Christians elsewhere. The Christian Highlander, they say, is employed in determining whether he is a true servant of Christ or not, when he should be proving that he is so by being "up and doing." The same amount of religious principle, because of this subjective tendency, is thought to throw off a less amount of work than otherwise it would. It is to the same source the peculiar order and position of "the men" is ultimately traced. It is an excessive self-suspiciousness, say they of the south, that has originated the fellowship meeting, and there "the men" acquired their position and influence. The same peculiarity finds another development in the paucity of communicants in the Highlands. It is affirmed that there they frighten themselves by an exaggerated standard of fitness, and are guided by their feelings rather than by the written Word. Thus all the peculiarities of the type of religion prevalent in the Highlands are traced to one source; and would be designated by those who are unfriendly the gloominess, the bigotry, and the closetism of Highland Christians, the undue influence of "the men," and the extreme paucity of communicants.

1. The gloominess of Highland Christians is unfairly taken for granted, and on the ground of the assumption, some of their Lowland brethren have been forward to denounce them. All that there is of truth in this charge is, that they were free from frivolity. They were grave, but not gloomy. They had not the light cheerfulness of unbroken hearts. They did not, like others, take it for granted that they were "the Lord's," they could not, like others, speak peace to themselves; but, unlike many others, they were dependent on the Lord for their hope and their joy. If some of those who denounce their gloominess were as willing as they were to dispense with all joy not the "fruit of the Spirit," they would regard with less complacency their own state of feeling; and if they had more true godliness, and some common sense, they would refrain from casting aspersions on the memories of these men of God. As they are, they cannot sympathise with the broken-hearted who join trembling with their mirth. Always on the surface, alike of their hearts and their Bibles, they may feel that they are masters of their happiness; but it ill becomes them to cast their shafts at those to whose depths of distress, under a sense of corruption, He only can bring peace who "searcheth the deep things of God."

It cannot be denied that the pious Highlander was wont to look within. To do so cannot always be a mistake. If the Christian looks within for the warrant of his faith, he of course greatly errs. If he looks to his own state of feeling as his rule of duty, instead of being always guided by the word of command from his Master, again he greatly errs. But would it not be an error greater still not to look within at all? Is there no prayerful watchfulness over his heart which it is his duty to practise? Ought he not to examine himself, habitually and closely, in order to ascertain the state and progress of his soul? Must he not keep an eye on his spirit while engaged in his work, lest his service should be found by the Lord to be a graceless formality? While the Christian is on earth there will be flesh as well as spirit in him; and in the flesh a love of ease, causing a constant tendency in his soul to subside into a state of stagnancy. He who resists not this tendency may present a smooth surface of hopefulness which, though but a covering over deadness and decay, may seem in favourable contrast to the disquietude of those who are more deeply stirred by a sense of corruption, more aware of their own deceitfulness, more moved by the solemn realities of eternity, and therefore less forward to declare their hope. But is the stillness of the former safer or more healthful than the disquiet of the latter? Will there not be more of genuine faith mingled with the groanings of the one than is expressed in the easy assurance of the other?

The Highland Christian cannot account for the ease with which a Lowlander, of whose piety he is persuaded, can adopt the language of assurance in his addresses to God. It is such a habit that he thinks the confidence with which his brother speaks cannot always be in his heart, and if it is not there, he cannot, he thinks, be right in using words which express it. And when he speaks with assurance, in the name of a mixed multitude, in public prayer, he cannot conceive how he can be speaking honestly. He could not speak thus dishonestly himself, and this is just the difference between the two. And is there not good reason for affirming that there is as great a tendency to an arid objectiveness on the one side, as to a morbid subjectiveness on the other, to an unlicensed familiarity on the one side, as to a slavish distrust on the other.

The Christians in the Highlands had been taught to distinguish between doubting the safety of their state and doubting the truth of the Word. They were accustomed to hear that one may be trusting in Christ while continuing to feel that he is a sinner, and without any evidence at all of his yet being a saint. It was not the same kind of evidence they required to satisfy them as to the trustworthiness of Christ, as they needed to assure them of being partakers of His grace. They had learned to be content with the Word as the

Open air service at Ferintosh Burn about 1843. (Reproduced from an old postcard)

REVD. THOMAS HOG,
1628 - 1692.

THE ORIGINAL INSCRIPTION ON THE
TOMBSTONE BELOW IS AS FOLLOWS :

"THIS STONE SHALL BEAR WITNESS
AGAINST THE PARISHIONERS OF
KILTEARN IF THEY BRING ANE
UNGODLY MINISTER IN HERE."

1940.

The memorial plaque which reproduces the partly defaced inscription on Thomas Hog's tombstone at the entrance to Kiltearn Church.

The Parish Church at Redcastle, Killearnan where Dr Kennedy's father, Rev. John Kennedy, was minister from 1813 to 1841.

Kiltearn Parish Church, near Evanton, where Thomas Hog was minister from 1654 until his death in 1692. Note the stone steps to the pulpit door on the gable.

evidence of the former, but they sought in their "life and conversation" for the evidence of the latter. They could quite understand why Christ, who so often reproved His disciples for their unbelief, should yet excite them to self-jealousy when He said — "One of you is a devil," and "One of you shall betray me," and why Peter, to whom a special message of comfort had previously been sent, should thrice be asked, "Lovest thou me?" If some others understood this as well, the case of the Highland Christian would not be such a puzzle to them as it seems to be.

There are some who, once obtaining somehow a hope of safety, banish all fears as to their interest in Christ from their hearts. A hope of being safe is all they desire, and having this they seek not for evidence of being holy. There are some Christians, too, who are strangers to the anxieties of others of their brethren, just because they are less impressed by the reality of eternal things, and less acquainted with the deceitfulness, as well as less pained by the corruption of their hearts. These would have no sympathy with the godly Highlander who shrinks from expressing an assurance of his interest in Christ. They would attribute his fears to mistaken views and to an unhealthy state of feeling. They cannot conceive how he can be at all trusting in Christ, while at the same time not assured of his interest in Him. They seem to think that the individual's interest in Christ, as surely as his right to appropriate Him, is matter of direct revelation. They forget that the persuasion I may trust in Christ is one thing, the consciousness that I am trusting in Him another thing, and the assurance that I have trusted in Him yet another still. One may surely have the first without the second, and one may have the first and second without the third. The believer may be trusting in Christ, and yet not assured that he is. He may be conscious of an exercise of trust, and yet be suspecting the genuineness of his faith. This suspicion is not to be rudely put down, as if it were the working of unbelief or the fruit of temptation. It may prove to be a healthful feeling; profitable as it moves one to examine the fruits of his faith, and hurtful only when it degenerates into a slavish fear, under the power of which the soul departs from the Lord.

It would indeed be false to affirm that there were no extreme developments of the Highland peculiarity, in the case both of individuals and communities, in the north, but it would be quite as false to affirm that these were the results of the kind of preaching for which the eminent ministers of Ross-shire were distinguished. Never, since the Apostles' day, was the foundation more wisely laid than by these preachers of the Gospel, and by none was its own place more carefully reserved for the written Word of God; but, at the same time, they were careful to distinguish between "the wood, hay, and stubble," and the "gold and precious stones" of the superstructure, and anxious to keep Christians dependent on grace, and alive to the importance of things unseen and eternal. A Christian, moulded after the fashion of their teaching, would be a man who, after a thorough work of conviction, found himself hopeless in "the horrible pit," and helpless in "the miry clay," and quite at the disposal of the Sovereign who "will have mercy on whom he will"; who was raised by the quickening Spirit, and established on the "Rock of Ages," and was thenceforth learning more and more to seek his righteousness and his strength in Christ, who, with clear views of the doctrines of the Gospel, combines an earnest desire to feel more of its power, who is kept sensible of heart-plagues, and is not allowed to be ignorant of Satan's devices; who is anxious rather to be spiritual than to be merely busy in his generation-work; who, as he cannot take his own Christianity for granted, is not easily satisfied with the profession of others, but who, while severe in his judgment of himself, and afraid to spoil an inquirer by premature comforts, is all warmth and tenderness of heart to all in whom there is seen "some good thing toward the Lord." There were many Highlanders among the Christians of whom aught of this, and there were some Christians among the Highlanders of whom all of this, could not be affirmed; but such was the genuine Highland Christian as reared under the ministry of the Ross-shire Fathers.

2.   There have been exhibitions in the North of a spirit of proud exclusiveness, but the staple Christianity of Ross-shire was never smitten by it. It is not a peculiarity of any one country that its

Christians find it more difficult to recognise true godliness in any other development than in that of the type to which they have been accustomed. This has often made a pious Highlander cautious in meeting the advances of a Christian from the south, who was too prone to regard his carefulness as the sternness of bigotry. This caution, and the habit of keeping his eye on the Bible standard of godliness, may have given an air of exclusiveness to his bearing towards others; but he never was one-half so severe upon them as he was always accustomed to be upon himself. He had learned, in travelling over his native hills, when about to leave the beaten track, to plant his foot firmly before him, and to refrain from advancing till he had examined the ground over which he was to pass. He had too often fallen into quagmires not to be cautious when treading where they abound. But he had known, too, so much of his own deceitfulness, and so often found a fair profession to be a false one, that he also learned to be cautious in his advances towards them who are called by the name of the Lord.

3.   Under the vague charge to which the name of Closetism has been given — just because it was never distinctly designated before, and because it can only be appropriately, when vaguely named — there are hid insinuations of licentiousness and indolence. It is suspected by some that the religion of the Highlands is something which the possessors never bring out of their closets but to pit it against the religion of others. There never was a fouler calumny than this. Nowhere could Christians be found more intolerant of Antinomianism, in themselves or in others, than the godly Highlanders; more careful to order their households in the fear of the Lord; more exact in their dealings in the market-place, and more circumspect in their whole life and conversation.

It is true, they may not have had the activity of those who delight in the bustle of mere surface work in public, but they were not idle in the house of the Lord. Neither was their place there a mere subordinate one, nor their work such as bore with no effect on the advancement of the cause of the Redeemer. Their work was less seen than that of others, whose labours were chiefly on the outside of the tabernacle. Their work was more hidden, for they wrestled in "the holiest." There they were taking no rest to themselves, and they were giving no rest to the Lord, and no contribution of service to the work of the Lord could be more precious than theirs, who were moving by prayer the very arm of Omnipotence.

The chief care of the Ross-shire Fathers was to raise a godly seed. Personal Christianity was the great object on which their attention and their labour were bestowed. They were not anxious merely to spread a layer of religion thinly over the face of society, but to obtain, from the Lord's hand, living specimens of the power of His grace. They were anxious, too, to employ in the work of the Lord only such as were prepared by Himself. There did not attend the progress of their work the outward bustle, arising from the wanton multiplication of agents, and of means that in other places may have got up a superficial religious excitement. Now-a-days the chief care seems to be expended on the construction of a social Christianity. Personal godliness is not so carefully required as in the days of the Fathers. If there be no overt ground for suspecting the religion of an individual, a place and work will be given him in the house of the Lord. The stones that seem at all in shape are taken as they are and placed in the building. No care being taken in selecting and in hewing, much building work is done. Ordinary decency being all that is required to secure them employment, many agents are at work about the house of the Lord. But, in reality, how little may after all be achieved!

Of the two kinds of labour, that of the Ross-shire Fathers was the safer and the more efficient. The living stones did find their place, and the spiritual priesthood their work in the temple of the Lord, but not so many more besides as to hide and overwhelm them; and the progress of the building, if not noisy and rapid, was solid and sure. But out of the mass of building carelessly raised after a different system how few living stones, and out of a multitude of workmen hastily collected how few spiritual priests may in the day of trial be found? A seemingly thriving and a really active church may be the embodiment of a great practical lie.

It was only in defence of the blessed memory of the righteous that a comparison has been drawn between the type of religion peculiar to the north and that which prevails in the south. Instead of doing so to provoke animosity and debate, it were better, while accepting the genuine in all its developments, to admire the wisdom of the Lord as displayed in the variety. If the peculiarity of the Celtic temperament and of the Celtic piety unfitted the godly Highlander for the activities of a more public position, the Lord whom he served did not call him to go forth; and if in the more uniform hopefulness of the Christian Lowlander there is aptness for employment so uncongenial to the other, the Lord has assigned him his position in a more bustling sphere. But if his father keeps a David at home while Eliab is in arms on the battlefield, let not the praying shepherd boy forget his brother in the fight, nor let the warrior in his armour despise the stripling with his sling, for when the victory has been won, his hand will be found to have done more than his own to achieve it.

4.   The fellowship meeting was a very early product of the vital Christianity of the Highlands. It arose spontaneously out of the lively feeling pervading the first groups of believers there. We cannot conceive of a party of exercised Christians met together without some converse regarding the fruits and evidences of true godliness. Such converse would naturally arise if there was any unsuspecting interchange of thoughts in their intercourse. One of them would be sure to have his doubts and difficulties; these he would state to his brethren, and they, from the Word of God and their own experience, would endeavour to afford him suitable counsel and comfort. Finding such converse to be edifying, and remembering that Christians are exhorted to comfort and to edify one another, what would be more likely than that they should set apart seasons for that duty, that He who gave the counsel might have to record the fact, "even as also ye do." In order to conduct the exercise in an orderly way, what would be more likely than that they should choose him whom they accounted the most advanced among them to preside over them, and that he should ask each one who could do so to speak to the question in course? Thus the fellowship meetings would be at last set up. Why should not the minister then adopt it, and, by taking the direction into his own

hands, do all he could to provide for its being conducted "decently and in order"? And this is just the story of the rise and establishment of the Highland Fellowship Meeting. It was the product, not of the peculiar natural temperament of Highlanders, but of the lively spiritual feeling of Christians, fostered by the warm brotherly love that prevailed in the days of its origin. It is an interesting fact that on one of the slopes of the Pyrenees, where the Lord has reserved a small remnant of living Christians to Himself, conventicles exactly corresponding to the fellowship meetings of the Highlands of Scotland are held, the only differences being that there they "speak to the question" in French and not in Gaelic, and that they have no minister to patronise and direct them. So naturally, indeed, do such meetings arise out of a healthful state of religious feeling that the communities in which they are awanting are those from whom an apology is required.

5.   The most evident peculiarity yet remains to be considered, the paucity of communicants in Highland congregations. Lowlanders trace this to an unhealthy state of feeling on the part of the people, and to unwise teaching on the part of the ministers. Both people and ministers are thus put on their defence.

It would seem, at first sight, more likely that the different state of matters in the south should be right. The great men and the learned are there, and those who differ from them may be supposed to be mistaken. But what if it should be otherwise? There were great men and good in the north who thought so; and the fact that the godly ministers in the Highlands possessed such influence in moulding the views and habits of the people, and such facility in carrying on the Lord's work according to their own ideal, is a reason why a defence of them is the more necessary, and is, at the same time, a strong stimulus and encouragement to attempt it. It would, indeed, be more than unwise, out of blind reverence for the Fathers, to take for granted that all must be right which we have received from their hand. It would be unsafe and insane to close one's eyes before the halo of their piety and to accept without inquiry all that they have given us; but it would be casting contempt on men, who have claims to our profoundest respect, to take for granted that they were wrong because their practice was exceptional; and his would be a craven heart who would shrink from their defence if he judged them to be right.

They of the south maintain that both the sacraments, being seals of the same covenant, and imposing the self-same obligations, ought to be administered on the same footing, the same kind and measure of profession and of qualification being required on the part of applicants for either; that no adult should be admitted to the one without being admitted also to the other; and that the Christian profession required of a parent, in order to the baptism of his child, cannot be complete without his being a communicant. The result of these views being carried into practice in the Lowlands, or rather the result of their mode of reducing them to practice, is that, with rare exceptions, all the members of a congregation above a certain age go to the table of the Lord, and that any parent who is a communicant receives, as a matter of course, baptism for his child.

The Ross-shire Fathers held that though in general the two sacraments were equally seals of the covenant of grace, they do in some respects differ even as sealing ordinances; that baptism, being the door of admission into the visible Church, a larger exercise of charity is required in dealing with applicants for that sacrament than is called for in administering the other, which implies a confirmation of those who were members before; that the lessons of baptism are more elementary than those of the sacrament of the Supper; that the connection of the child and of both the parents, with an ordinary case of infant baptism, calls for peculiar tenderness on the part of Church rulers, and that the rule of Scripture requires baptism to be given on an uncontradicted profession of faith, while an accredited profession is required to justify the Church in granting admission to the table of the Lord. The result of carrying these views into practice is well known; the number of members in full communion is comparatively small, and parents who have never communicated receive baptism for their children.

The Ross-shire Fathers of course held that the two sacraments were in *general* seals of the covenant of grace, and that as such they were equally valid. But they also held with Mastricht that they did not *specially* seal the same measure of privilege. They regarded baptism as the sacrament of admission, specially sealing the believers' introduction into the covenant of grace, and his interest in the initial blessings of regeneration and justification, and formally admitting him into the general membership of the visible Church. They regarded the Lord's Supper as the sacrament of nurture, specially sealing the believer's right to all that is required to advance him to "the stature of a perfect man in Christ Jesus," and formally admitting him when first administered into full communion with the Church, as one who, by the seeming fruits of his faith, had established his claims to the Church's confidence. They also held that in the professions required from applicants there must be a corresponding difference; the profession in either case being suitable to what is specially sealed by the sacrament for which they apply — an applicant for baptism making a suitable profession when declaring his faith in Christ, and specially his willingness to receive Him as his Saviour, and his resolution to serve Him as his Lord; but that a person desiring to communicate must profess not merely the first exercise of faith in Christ, but a persuasion or a hope derived from an examination of his experience and his life, that his faith is that which "worketh by love," "purifieth the heart," and "overcometh the world." They, moreover, held that there must be a corresponding difference in the actions of the Church in administering the sacraments — that the Church ought to sustain, in the case of a person applying for baptism either for himself or for his child, a profession not made incredible by ignorance and immorality, but that none ought to be admitted to the Lord's table in whom, after examination, tenderly and wisely conducted, no seeming evidence of grace can at all be discerned; or, as Dr Macdonald was accustomed to state it, applicants for baptism should be admitted on an *uncontradicted*, and applicants for the other sacrament on an *accredited*, profession of faith.

There are here three distinct statements: the first, defining the distinctive characters of the two sacraments; the second, describing the profession required on the part of applicants for either; and, the third, laying down the rule of the Church's duty in dealing with these applicants. If the position assumed in the first of these statements is tenable, the defence of the others is secured. But let it once be determined that there is no such difference between the two sacraments, as has been indicated, and it will be impossible to hold the position that they ought not to be administered by the Church on the very same footing, or that she should require a different profession and a higher qualification from applicants in the case of the one than she insists on in the case of the other. But if the distinctive characters of the two sacraments be such, as the Ross-shire Fathers were accustomed to define them, the practical distinction observed in their mode of administering them can be triumphantly defended. And yet it would seem an easy thing to defend the first point of attack, though one cannot but suspect that something is overlooked in examining the position, and that this accounts for the confidence with which it is scanned when he looks to the hosts across the Spey who are marshalled against him.

It is not denied that baptism is a seal of the covenant of grace, and that an interest in all the blessings of that covenant is secured to the believer at the moment of his union to Christ. Nor is it denied that the blessings which are said to be specially sealed to the believer by baptism are an earnest of all spiritual blessings in heavenly places. At the same time, it is held that the blessings of regeneration and justification alone are directly presented in baptism to the understanding and faith of the believer, and that it was the divine intention, as declared in the divine Word, specially to seal by this sacrament an interest in these blessings alone. (Rom. 6: 1-4; Col. 2: 12; Acts 2: 38). It is difficult to see how, without this limitation of its special effect as a seal, baptism, once for all, is sufficient. The fact that it is administered only once to the same individual is instructive and necessary according to the view of it now given. It teaches the consoling truths that once in Christ the believer is for ever in Him; that once regenerated he is for ever spiritually alive, and that once justified he is for ever free from condemnation.

If these blessings alone are specially sealed by baptism, how and when is an interest in them obtained? At the moment of the soul's union to Christ, and, in the case of an adult, when he first exercises faith in Jesus. If so, this act of faith is what an applicant for baptism must profess. He may at once, yea, he ought immediately to profess it; and on that profession he may be "baptised straightway." Such was the profession on which the Pentecost converts, the Eunuch, the Philippian jailer, and Lydia were baptised. It was the invariable rule to sustain such a profession in the days of the Apostles. They did so not as men inspired to judge infallibly the state of those who applied to them. Instead of this, they refrained from forming any positive judgment regarding the state of professing believers. They acted as wise men, but as mere men and charitable, not as inspired men and infallible; and, casting the responsibility on those who made it, they administered baptism on an uncontradicted profession of faith. Proof that they were not infallible is furnished by every reported case of apostasy, and proof that they did not venture to pass judgment on the state of applicants is clearly furnished in Paul's method of dealing with the Philippian jailer. What but a merely uncontradicted profession of faith could there have been in the case of one whose conversion could only have occurred a few minutes before? He "was baptised, he and all his, straightway." There was no opportunity of knowing him by his fruits. He professed to have just believed in Christ, and there being nothing known to forbid the hope that his profession was genuine, he was at once baptised. Now, if it was the same profession that was required by the Apostles for the baptism of oneself, as for the baptism of his child, and if it was and could only be such, as the "charity" that "thinketh no evil" alone could accept, was not this exactly the practice of the Ross-shire Fathers in administering that ordinance?

It may be objected, however, that the profession of a parent educated under the Gospel ought to embrace more than that of a recent convert. We ought, indeed, to expect more knowledge in the former case; but, if that is competent, and if his conduct furnishes no positive evidence against him, why should not his profession of faith be accepted? And there is in his case a reason why it should, not found in the case of one claiming baptism for himself. He is already a member of the Church, and as "the infants of such as are members of the visible Church are to be baptised,'' on no ground can the baptism of his child be refused that will not justify the Church in excommunicating or suspending him. The fact of his not being a communicant is held in the south to be a sufficient reason for refusing the baptism of his child. If it be so, it must be a good reason for at least suspending him from the enjoyment of all the privileges of his status, as a member of the Church. To refuse baptism is but to take that suspension for granted, when there is no such act of the Church to which to refer. And the strange thing is, that the very man who would be punished, to the extent of disallowing his membership altogether, would be, at the very same time, rewarded with both the sacraments, if he would take them! The one, which demands the larger exercise of charity in its administration, is refused, but both would be given him at once! He, who is on the eve of being excluded from the pale of the Church, will be welcomed into the full communion of the Church, if he will only offer himself to her embrace!

It may be said that, by not accepting of both the sacraments, he proves himself unfit for either of them. This might be allowed, if it might be taken for granted that in absenting himself from the Lord's table he indicated a wilful contempt of Christ's authority and a wanton neglect of His ordinance. But surely this is not always the case; and we are firmly persuaded that such a feeling as often finds expression in the conduct of those who go to the table of the Lord as in that of many in the north who refrain from communicating; the difference between some of either class being simply this — the former, being dead to all the solemn considerations suggested by the ordinance of the Supper, are bold to go forward, while the latter, having some sensitiveness of conscience, shrink from approaching the table of the Lord, fearing that it is neither legitimate nor safe for them to do so.

It is altogether unfair to charge on the Ross-shire Fathers any remissness in requiring from parents the due discharge of their duties towards their children. They were careful to seek security to the Church for ''the godly upbringing of the young''; but this they obtained more effectually than by making each parent a communicant, by taking pains in private and public catechising to teach them the doctrines of grace, and the requirements of the law of the Lord. The plain truth is that they were invariably more strict in administering baptism than their brethren in the south, who differed from them mainly in this — that while opening the door of admission more widely than they, these laid the other sacrament in front of it, not as a barrier against the rush of the multitude, but as a broad stepping-stone to facilitate their access.

The views of the sacrament of the Supper, and the practice in administrating it, which are peculiar to the north, remain to be considered. The difference between it and the other sacrament, insisted on by the ministers in the Highlands, has been already pointed out. This distinction was clearly seen and firmly acted on by the Ross-shire Fathers. They were fully persuaded in their own minds as to this matter. They had no difficulty in regarding the sacrament of the Supper, as intended by the Lord, specially to seal something other and higher than that which is specially sealed by baptism. They called it, with Mastricht, *"sacramentum nutritionis,"* as being intended to be an occasional feast to believers during all their wilderness journey. They beheld in the symbols of Christ's body and blood the clearest and the closest manifestation of the glory of the Lord, and in the exercise of those who partake of them the nearest approach to the Lord that can be on the earth. They regarded the guests at that table as having the most conspicuous connection with the cause and glory of Christ. They saw the Church pointing the eye of the world to a communion table, to inform them whom she accredited as the true people of God. On all these accounts they felt that they were specially called to guard the passage to the table of the Lord, and to subject to the closest scrutiny all who would approach it. And surely they were right. And if they were, how can an indiscriminate, a wholesale, admission to this sacrament be justified, when the mass is just as heterogeneous as that with which they had to deal?

As to the propriety of carefulness in granting admission to the table of the Lord, as a matter of opinion, there will be no dispute, whatever may be the difference in practice. Those who condemn the mode of administering the sacraments followed in the north must insist that there is no more urgent call to fence the table of the Lord than there is to guard the sacrament of baptism. If they can establish this from the nature of the two sacraments, and from the Word of God, they may prove the Ross-shire practice to be wrong; but just as surely as they do so, they will fail in showing that their own is right. If there is an equally urgent call to be careful in the case of both, they may prove it is not right to make a distinction in administering them; but they cannot surely make out, what would be the only justification of their own practice, that it is right not to be careful as to either. But the former they will fail, and the latter they won't try, to prove.

It is surely unnecessary to furnish any proof of the statement that both the sacraments do not specially seal the same blessings, though both are, in general, equally seals of the covenant of grace. If it were not so, it would be impossible to show why there should be two; a second would be quite superfluous if it specially sealed no more than the first; but surely there is no redundancy where only two are acknowledged and administered. If baptism seals the believer's introduction into the covenant, and his interest in the blessings bestowed on him immediately on his union to Christ, and if these blessings are an earnest of all "spiritual blessings in heavenly places," the other sacrament directly seals his right to all of which he had a sealed earnest given to him before. The Lord's Supper as a seal was intended to assure believers of their interest in all that was required to prepare them for glory, and as a feast was appointed to be a means of applying that provision to their souls.

It is difficult to conceive how any serious objection could be offered to this representation of its use. "This cup," saith Christ, "is the New Testament in my blood," the fulness of the blessings of that covenant as procured by His blood, being by these words, in explanation of the symbol, specially represented and sealed to believers. In only one of the four descriptions given in Scripture of the mode of celebrating the Lord's Supper is there any mention of the blessing of pardon, and there it is not spoken of as if specially sealed at the time. It is only referred to in such a way as to intimate that it was unnecessary specially to seal it, this having formerly been done. "This is my blood of the New Testament, which is shed for *many* for the remission of sins." In these words Christ mentions it in a doctrinal statement, to explain how the provision of the covenant was secured to His people by His blood, and what was the divinely appointed order in which that provision was applied. *Their* justification is taken for granted, and the abstract blessing is pointed to, only in its place in the arrangements of the covenant, as an earnest of all other spiritual blessings, and the benefits, of which it is an earnest, are alone directly represented and specially sealed.

If it seals a more advanced privilege, it teaches a higher lesson than baptism. It presents to us the mystery of Christ's person, and the mystery of Christ's death, in relation to the everlasting covenant of grace. Deeply did the disciples feel that these lessons were not easily learned. In presence of no other does a living soul feel more dependent on divine teaching than when before the lesson of the words, "This is my body which is broken for you." And who, being one of the "disciples indeed," will deny that he is only slowly creeping on his way to the high attainment of tracing his salvation, entirely and closely, to the death of Christ as its only channel, and to the covenant love of Jehovah, as its primary source? In baptism, on the other hand, Christ is represented in the general aspect of His office as a Saviour from sin, and its lessons are those which are given to the class of beginners — our need of cleansing from sin; Christ as the only "fountain opened for sin and uncleanness"; the necessity of an interest in Him; the infallible certainty of salvation to all who are found in Him; and the obligation resting on all who believe in His name to "walk in newness of life."

And surely those who are admitted to the table of the Lord are placed in closer and more manifest connection with the cause and the glory of the Lord than they ever were before. Even if the Lord's Supper were nothing more than a second seal it would have this effect. All the more, if it specially seals an advance of privilege. He who comes to the table of the Lord must come nearer than before to the Lord of the table. At the great love-feast there spread, the guests are seated, as at the family table, in the House of the King, and those who admit them point the eye of the world to them as the accredited children of Zion. Of the merely baptised they may say, "These have come into the house of the Lord, but we merely admitted them, in the charitable hope that they might prove what they professed to be." But of these others they must say, "We have tried them, and we accredit them as approved followers of Christ."

Is there not then good ground for maintaining that the way to the table of the Lord ought to be more strictly guarded than the outer door of His house? Must not the applicant for admission to it profess that he has been regenerated and justified already? Can he sit down at a feast without professing that he lives, has appetite for the food placed before him, and has an invitation from Him by whom it was provided? Is he not expressly commanded to examine himself as to these things, "and so," and only so, "to eat of that bread and drink of that cup"? And can the Church deal faithfully with him without instituting a closer scrutiny than before into his knowledge, experience, and conduct, when he is now extending his profession and taking a nearer position to the Lord among His followers on earth? Can the Church be faithful to her Head without doing so? And was not this all that was done by the Ross-shire Fathers, though a supercilious sneer is very often the only notice taken of their conduct?

Whatever opinion may be formed of the grounds on which the practice of the Ross-shire Fathers was defended, it certainly has the advantage of being *the only mode according to which the rulers of the Church can suitably express their varied feelings towards applicants for sealing ordinances.* There will always be about the Church those who may be excluded and in the Church those who may be extruded without any breach of charity. Against these let the door of admission be shut. Within the Church also there have always been those who make a profession of religion which cannot be summarily rejected, but which can win no unsuspecting confidence. Let such be allowed to remain within her pale, but into full communion let them not be admitted. Let only such as have accredited their profession be received within the inner circle, by the sealing ordinance of the Supper. This is the only course of

procedure on the part of Church rulers that can be suitable in
relation to the three classes with whom they have invariably to
deal; and this was the practice of the Ross-shire Fathers. Acting on
their views of the distinctive characters of the two sacraments, they
enjoyed a liberty in dispensing ordinances, which they cannot have
who, acting according to different views, are under the painful
constraint of being compelled either to exclude an applicant from
membership altogether, or to admit him within the innermost circle
around the table of the Lord.

Am I not justified in cherishing the hope of their being Christians
regarding some professors whom I cannot confidently embrace as
brethren in the Lord? Ought I to admit them into intimate fellowship till I become more satisfied than I am as to their acquaintance
with the power of godliness? Surely I am not required summarily to
reject all whom I cannot confidently receive as Christians, nor to be
on terms of intimate fellowship with all whom, in the judgment of
charity, I regard as such. And why should not the same liberty be
allowed to the Church? Is she bound to exclude from her pale all
whom into full communion she cannot admit? Yet much would be
her bondage if the two sacraments were to be administered on the
same footing. But such fetters were never placed by Christ's hand
on the conscience of the Church. They who are in the state of
bondage have themselves forged their chains.

The practice peculiar to the North has another marked advantage:
*it is admirably adapted to meet the various feelings of applicants for
sealing ordinances.* When a Christian applies for admission to the
table of the Lord, who is enabled to express a hope of an interest in
Christ, and in whom some seeming marks of grace are discerned, at
once, but not because any judgment of his state has been formed,
his request is complied with. But among true Christians there have
always been differences as to the measure of their hope. All of them
incline to seek communion with the Church, but some of them can
only come with a trembling heart to ask for the privilege. One of
these comes to a pious Highland minister in olden times to speak to
him about communicating. Does the minister insist on his expressing
an assurance of his conversion before he grants him admission to

the table of the Lord? Does he require him to satisfy him by a record of his experience that the change through which he passed was really spiritual and saving? Not at all. How then does he act? He examines him closely, but wisely and tenderly; and in the measure in which he finds such views and feelings as seem to indicate a work of grace in his soul, he labours to remove his difficulties, and offers him all needed counsel and encouragement when giving him a token of admission to the table of the Lord.

Let us suppose this man under the *regime* of the south. Not being a communicant he is in the judgment of the Church there no member of the Church at all. His status as a member of the Church, because of his own baptism in infancy, is disallowed; although, by no formal act of the Church, had he ever been deprived of it. He will be acknowledged as a member only if he communicates; although at the time he is a member of the mystical body of Christ, and had been admitted into the visible Church by baptism before! The sacrament of the Supper is thus made the door of admission to the Church! By a very mysterious process of transposition, the inner becomes at once the outer door of the house of the Lord! Let us further suppose that this man is a parent, and that he is applying for the baptism of his child. Meeting with no one to sympathise with his scruples as to the other sacrament, and no effort made to remove them, he resolved not to ask a token of admission to the table of the Lord. He is asked if he is a communicant, and simply because he says he is not, and cannot promise to become one, the privilege for which he asks is refused. This refusal rests on a denial of his being a member of the Church. No minister, it is presumed, would refuse to baptise the infant of a parent, who himself had just been baptised, before he had at all partaken of the sacrament of the Supper. The Apostles, we know, did not refuse to do so. Baptism conferred, in their judgment, the privilege of membership in the visible Church. Because the parent thus became a member, his child also was baptised. But refuse the applicant in the supposed case, and you act towards the man on the assumption that he is not a member of the Church at all; and you thrust out that timid child of God beyond the pale of the Church because he has not yet the courage to ask for admission into full communion.

The following case has actually occurred: A Highlander, temporarily residing in a Lowland district, applies to a minister for the baptism of his child. He is one of that minister's most regular hearers. The elders report him as correct in all his habits. He is, in fact, the only one in the district in which he resides who maintains the worship of God in his family, though his neighbours are all communicants. But because he cannot declare that he is, nor promise to become a communicant, he is summarily dismissed. After him comes to the study a man from whom his children often heard an oath, but from whom they never yet heard a prayer, and who seldom returned sober from a market; but he is a communicant, and, of course, his child is baptised the very next Sabbath!

Let us suppose the case of one whose profession is really false, though his knowledge is competent and his known habits correct. He applies to a Lowland minister for the baptism of his infant. He has himself a suspicion that matters are not right between his soul and the Lord, but he is anxious that his child should be baptised. In order to obtain that he smothers his scruples, and agrees to become a communicant. What effect will this have on the mind and heart of the man? What must he think of the minister who will insist on his taking both the sacraments, while he himself is aware that he is unfit for either of them? With what feelings will he receive the highest attestation of his profession which the Church has thus thrust upon him, while his own conscience testifies to its falseness? And how will his communicating affect his soul? He will have borne down all his rising scruples, and left the communion table under the judgment of increased hardness of heart. If he had to do with one of the Ross-shire Fathers, the privilege he first sought would not, indeed, have been withheld from him. In such a case it could not, as there was no overt contradiction of his profession of faith by his conduct. The minister would remember, too, that if either parent was a believer the child must be "holy"; and that the probabilities as to both father and mother must be taken into account, as well as the interest of the child; and, therefore, after serious dealing with his conscience, and casting the responsibility on himself, he would agree to baptise his child. But he would do no more. This is all the account he makes of man's profession. His giving him the baptism of his child was doing as much as the man's profession would bear, and his not offering him the other sacrament was a testimony on the side of conscience in the breast of him with whom he was dealing.

Four most desirable results were secured by the mode of dispensing sealing ordinances, practised in the north, which go far to prove that it was according to the mind, and was crowned with the blessing, of the Lord. (1) The Church was preserved from the extreme of exclusiveness on the one hand, and from that of laxity on the other. The door of admission was open to all whom "pity, charity, and prudence" would admit, and the inner circle was guarded from the profane rush of the crowd. (2) It marked and preserved a distinction, so far as this can be legitimately done, between the approved followers of Christ, and all others. This distinction, as an ecclesiastical one, is quite blotted out when both sacraments are administered on the same footing. (3) It kept up, in the conscience of non-communicants, a sense of shortcoming that would have been quite extinguished under a different system. (4) It always reminded the ministers of the danger of indiscriminate preaching, and secured some consistency between what was faithfully said in the pulpit and what was done in the session-house. When a minister has always a congregation of communicants before him, he is easily led to address them from the pulpit, as it ought to be fitting he should, when standing at the head of the table of the Lord. It is difficult to change one's form of addressing the same congregation, though standing on one occasion in the pulpit, and on another before it.

As to the prevalent feeling in the minds of Highlanders, in reference to the sacrament of the Supper, there has been much misconception in the south. It is supposed that the majority are utterly indifferent about it, and that some of the few pious people scare themselves away from it by superstitious notions of its sanctity. This is almost entirely a mistake. It might be an improvement on the state of matters elsewhere if all the communicants had as much respect for this ordinance as many of the non-communicants of the North, and took their way of expressing it; and it is the invariable experience of a Highland minister that all whom he would wish to bring forward do, sooner or later, apply for admission to the table of the Lord. It is often said that it is a sin not to confess Christ before men by obeying his dying command. His must be a most unhealthy state of feeling who, without a disquieting sense of guilt, can refrain from doing so. This cannot be denied; but let it not be forgotten that the sin which should in the first instance be felt is not his absenting himself from the table of the Lord, but his not coming to the Lord of the table. His error lies in his not coming to Christ that he might be entitled to communicate. The lack of faith in his first want and profession cannot surely supply it. And yet, if all are to be told without qualificaton that it is a sin not to communicate, the result would be a rush to the communion table to get rid of the uneasiness which such doctrine produces. And will not this be, in effect, to make profession a substitute for faith and a shelter for unbelief?

At least something might be said as an excuse for the state of feeling in the north in reference to the sacraments. Our enlightened friends in the south must not expect to find the body of the people in our dark region skilled to act on general principles, or so wise as to be guided otherwise than by simple and direct inferences from the Word of God, or so experienced as to have corrected their first impressions. And when a simple Highlander, without any formula to guide him in his study, takes up his Bible, to learn from it what the Lord says about this matter, and meets in it with no recorded instance of an unbeliever at the Lord's table, and ponders the solemn warnings by which it is guarded; when he contrasts the select companies who communicated with the crowds of whose baptism an account is given, and meets with no sanctions, around the one ordinance, that seem to compare with those by which the other is fenced, is it a wonder that this disciple should carry with him, from the perusal of the Bible, a more solemn impression of the one sacrament than of the other? If that man's state of feeling is not to be regarded with respect, let it not at least be treated with rudeness. And can we wonder that he, accustomed to see the southern practice followed by the Moderates around him, whom he regarded as ungodly men, never looking for guidance from on high, should have imagined that what he had originally derived from a study of the Word of God was confirmed to him by experience, that he should therefore have held his own views very firmly, and have looked with grave suspicion on the state of mind and feeling that differed from his own.

The Minister of Killearnan

PREFATORY NOTE

THE minister of Killearnan was my father. I could not forget this while I was writing this memoir. In the only sense in which he was my father, while he lived, I lost him when he died. But the memory of that loss I can bear to recall, as I cherish the hope that his death was the means of uniting us in bonds that shall never be broken. Doubly knit to him, therefore, now that he has gone, I can by no means keep down the son in my heart when I write or when I think of him. This accounts for the frequency with which ''I'' and ''my'' appear on the following pages. They came unconsciously from my pen, but when my eye detected them, they seemed so offensive that I was strongly induced to attempt their removal. But the effort to hide the son in the writer requiring the affectation of an indifference that was far from my feeling, both my heart and my conscience revolted against it. And, even if the change were permitted by these, my hand lacked the skill to make the change an improvement.

CHAPTER I

THE MINISTER OF KILLEARNAN

RISSEL, in the district of Kishorn, within the parish of Applecross, was my father's birthplace. It is one of those green spots that usually speck the breasts of hills, formed of such limestone rocks as abound in that part of the country. The time was when the most of these oases had cottages on or beside them. Often, throughout the Highlands, they now serve but to mark where cottages once stood. Some of these desolate hill-sides have seen better days, and they have their own striking way of telling their reverse. As one looks on them now, in their patched clothing of green and purple, through which the grey and naked elbows of the underlying rocks protrude, they seem like men of broken fortunes, wearing, all in rags, the dress of other days.

His father, himself the son of godly parents, was well known in the surrounding district. He had been educated with a view to the ministry, and had been for several sessions at college; but believing that the Lord had accepted his intention without requiring its fulfilment, as in the case of David in reference to the building of the temple, he never applied for licence, but lived to see two of his sons serving the Lord in the Gospel. Combining, with the warm heart of a Christian Highlander, an enlightened understanding and a tender conscience, he was a man to win affection and command respect. He was eminently a man of prayer; and such was the feeling with which, on that account, he was regarded by the people, that, when the fishermen were out on Loch Kishorn on a stormy night, they knew no fear so long as they saw the light in his window, believing that while it twinkled there he was pleading with God for their safety. During many years of his life he attended the ministry of Mr

Lachlan Mackenzie of Lochcarron, by whom he was greatly beloved and respected. Sometimes, when that godly minister would shrink from engaging in public duty, in a fit of unbelief, Donald Kennedy would succeed in persuading him, after all others had failed. Once, on the morning of a Communion Sabbath, when the hour for commencing the service had come, Mr Lachlan was still locked up in his bedroom. The morning had been stormy, and the Tempter had had found it easy to persuade him that this was permitted just to prevent his preaching, and that it would be presumption to go out in the face of a frowning providence. His friend from Kishorn had only arrived as the hour for beginning public worship had come. Being prepared to find, what he afterwards ascertained to be the case, he went at once to the minister's bedroom. The door was locked, and no answer would be given to all his knocks and entreaties. He had much in him yet of the strength of younger days, and, putting his shoulder to the door, he forced it open, and, on entering, found, as he expected, the minister stretched weeping on his bed. He ordered him at once, in accents tremulous with respect, to rise, telling him he was ashamed to find one who had so often caught the Tempter in a lie yielding yet again to his suggestions, and assuring him that if he went forward to the Lord's own work, at the Lord's own bidding, difficulties would vanish, and his fears be disappointed. Mr Lachlan yielded before his urgency, and scarcely had he crossed the threshold on his way to the place of meeting when the rain ceased, the clouds were scattered, and the frowning morning was succeeded by a smiling day of sunshine. During the service of that day the Lord's servants and people enjoyed a "time of refreshing" that left its mark on their memories for ever.

In his management of his household he was peculiarly conscientious. It was his habit, as it was that of "his father before him," when each of his children reached a certain age, to retire with them to a quiet spot in the wood, and there, after spending some time in prayer, after explaining to them the nature of his engagements in their behalf at their baptism, and appealing to their conscience as to his manner of fulfilling them, directing them to the only source of strength, he took them under vow to seek and serve the Lord. My father always retained a lively recollection of this solemn transaction.

But before that time, and even from his very infancy, he was regarded by his acquaintances as a subject of grace. At the age of three years it was his habit to retire to some secret place to pray. One day in his fourth year while thus engaged, a woman, who was passing, heard the child's voice lisping his petitions to God, and, arrested by the words she first heard, she stood to listen till his prayer was ended. What she then heard the Lord applied with saving power to her soul, and she, notorious only for wickedness before, was known from that time till her death as a consistent witness for God in the district. Thus early did the Lord give an earnest of the great usefulness of his later years.

Notwithstanding these indications of an earlier piety, he himself, sometimes at least, looked no further back than the twenty-fourth year of his age for the dawnings of spiritual life in his soul. In that year he passed through a process that gave him a deep experience of the convictions and temptations usually attending a work of conversion; but whether it availed merely to prepare him for dealing with the cases of others, or as his introduction into the kingdom of grace as well, it is now impossible conclusively to determine. But the individual himself not being always the best qualified to judge in such a case, I cannot dissent from the opinion of those who knew him in his youth, and who believed that he had feared the Lord from his earliest years.

About the sixth year of his age he was seized with small-pox. The attack proved to be very severe, and the child, unable to see or to speak, seemed lying at the very gates of death. Just when "at the lowest," and while his father was in his closet wrestling with God for his life, a man from the neighbourhood, who had the reputation of a seer, entered the house. The mother, ascertaining he was in, and having in her as much superstition as made her anxious to consult him, brought him to the room in which her son was lying. The child was quite aware of the man's entrance, but was utterly unable to express the horror with which his presence had inspired him. "What do you think of John?" asked the anxious mother.

The oracular reply was, "Ere the tide that now ebbs shall have touched the shore again, your child shall be no more." This the child distinctly heard, but it gave him no alarm. He knew the man who spake these words was a messenger of Satan, and the Lord so calmed his spirit that "the prince of the power of the air" could not stir it. Just then the father returned from his place of prayer, his face lighted up with the joy of hope. Observing the seer, he ordered him at once away. The man, too glad to escape, instantly vanished, though not through the chimney or the keyhole, as such persons were sometimes suspected of doing. Observing his wife in tears, he asked her why she was weeping. She told him the seer's gloomy prophecy. "The messenger of Satan lieth," he said; "the Lord hath given me the life of my child, the blessings of His right hand shall rest upon his head, and he shall yet serve the Lord in the gospel of His Son." In course of time the child recovered sight and health; but never could the man who prophesied his early death from that day look him in the face. He carefully avoided him whenever he seemed likely to meet him. But as he was leaving home on one of his journeys to college, and as he was passing out of a narrow gorge that formed the outlet of the glen behind his father's house, the seer suddenly came out from behind a rock, and, in a flutter of excitement, rushed up to him; but with no worse intent than to thrust a sum of money into his hand, which having done, he as suddenly again disappeared. Doubtless the man's conscience was smarting under a sense of guilt, and the money was intended as a solatium for the pain which he formerly inflicted.

His early education was the best that could be procured in the district. This, however, is no high praise. He was taught to read and write and count, and was crammed with Latin. This was all that parish teachers in the Highlands in those days usually tried to do, besides practising themselves in the use of the lash, their kilted pupils affording them a tempting facility for the performance. Each lesson given with this accompaniment left its mark on the skin as well as its print on the memory, and, it must be confessed, stuck well to the pupil. Better Latin scholars, at least, were turned out of the dreadful schools of those days than come from the pleasant seminaries of the present. Whatever was the character of the teacher under whom my father studied, he left his school prepared to pass respectably through the curriculum at King's College, Aberdeen.

Very different from what it now is was the journey to college in those days. Many students were obliged to walk their weary way from the far north to the Granite City. Sometimes a ghillie was in attendance, who carried the scanty wardrobe and the provisions for the way; a laird's son would have a horse and a ghillie. Hospitality was no rare virtue in the days of our fathers, and but few of the poor students had to pay for a night's lodging by the way. Some kind farmer was almost always found who made the weary traveller welcome to bed and board for a night. This might be less necessary to the student on his way to the south, his purse then containing the sum given him to meet the expenses of the session. But the purse was generally empty enough on his way home again. An Aberdeen professor used to tell his students of his having started once after a college session for his home in Caithness with only two pence in his pocket. On one of his journeys to college my father walked ''between sleep and sleep'' no fewer than eighty miles, a feat very unusual even in those pedestrian days.

A college life before his time was almost as unlike the present as were college journeys. Not long before then all the students occupied apartments within the college, and messed together. Strange parties these must have been that sat around the long table in the college hall! Many a district contributed its share of temper, fun, wildness, and awkwardness to the talk and the manners of that group of youths. Under a professor's eye and influence the whole might have been smoothed down into a very dull affair; but the recoil would be all the greater when the professor had gone, and wild and furious would be the din when each one in that motley group resumed his own proper phase, and found the reins lying on his neck again. Had the lodgings been comfortable, the fare good and cheap, and the supervision close and godly, this arrangement might have been excellent. Almost anything is better than to send a youth to college without a tutor or a friend, allowed to keep his own purse and to choose his own companions.

Three sessions then completed the literary course at King's College, and each professor carried a set of students through all the classes. This could only be a good arrangement if each professor was equally qualified in all the departments of study, if all were equally good or equally bad, and if the professor and his pupils took well to each other at the outset. But the ''Jack-of-all-trades'' is generally ''master of none''; and, considering the difficulty now felt in getting one suitable man for each Chair, we may not return to the plan requiring each professor to be qualified for all.

Two sessions only were then spent in the study of theology. Five years were thus the term of the youth's college studies for the ministry. This is now thought to be greatly too short; but if young men were only allowed to get out of their teens before entering college, the result of a five years' course would weigh just as much as that of eight years, on which a youth at twenty can now often look back. Let Greek and Latin and Hebrew be confined to schools and gymnasia, and let theological professors examine oftener and lecture less, and we can have in five years all that is worthy of a college in our present literary course, and quite as useful preparation for the work of the ministry as can now be procured in our divinity halls. But, after all, what avails any course of theological study if the essential qualification be awanting, which only the Spirit of the Lord can supply. It is too often supposed that any gifted man can be shaped into a minister, whereas the more talented a man is, and the more furnished with all the accessories that constitute a minister's intellectual equipment, the more dangerous will he prove if he be not a minister of God's own making. It is indeed a mistaken idea that learning is unnecessary and college studies useless; but it is a greater and more dangerous error so to elevate the importance of literature and science as practically, at least, to exalt them above the essential of godliness. On no account ought the Church to lower the standard of literary attainment by which candidates for the ministry are tried; but when she allows Satan so often to thrust ungodly men through her courts under the disguise which talent and learning may form, she should really be at liberty to receive occasionally from the Lord men whom He hath ''created anew'' for His work, though they may lack the trappings by which the ungodliness of these others was concealed. Sometimes such men have been signally blessed in the ministry of the gospel, and any arrangement that makes their reception impossible cannot be sanctioned by the Lord.

In these remarks some may think they discover an admission that my father's early education was defective. With all the ardour of my love to him and all the depth of my veneration for his memory, I will not claim for him any distinction for extraordinary talent or learning; nor does it pain me that I cannot. He may have entered college with the disadvantage of a defective education, and he may have passed into the hall without having made any marked progress in literature and science; but I can truly claim for him, at least, an ordinary measure of attainments. His sternly exclusive regard to what was substantial and useful made him utterly indifferent to the acquirement of what was merely shadowy or showy. He knew what he lacked, and if he chose he could acquire it; but if he was understood, this was all he was ever careful about, as to his manner of expressing his thoughts when preaching the gospel. The idea of studying manner or style was one that never found a place in his mind. But what a counterpoise to every defect in point of literary acquirement and mere superficial polish, were his sound and penetrating judgment, his devotion of heart to the service of the Lord, his experience from very infancy of the power of the truth, his habitual prayerfulness, and that holy watchfulness which communion with God never fails to produce. Such was my father when studying for the ministry, and if I may not be proud of him, I cannot be ashamed of him.

During the interval between two of his college sessions an incident occurred to which he often gratefully referred. He and his brother Neil, having gone a deer-stalking, they came in sight of a herd which they could only approach within gunshot by creeping slowly up the slope of a hill. John was in advance as they were stealing their way towards the deer. The trigger of his brother's gun having been caught by the heather, the shot was discharged, and the ball passed through his coat. Rising at once, he said to his brother, "Neil, I think it is time for us to give up this work."

Discharging his own gun, he shouldered it, and, on reaching home, laid it aside never to use it again.

He was licenced to preach the gospel by the Presbytery of Lochcarron, November 24th, 1795, in the twenty-fourth year of his age. His discourses, all of which he delivered that day, ''were unanimously approved of,'' and the Presbytery ''were fully satisfied with the manner in which he acquitted himself in the languages, moral and natural philosophy.'' Either at the same meeting, or nearly about the same time, other young men were licenced. Referring to the group, Mr Lachlan said, ''The others are only preachers of our making, but the Lord made a preacher of John Kennedy.''

About the time of his licence he was appointed teacher of the Parish School of Lochcarron. While discharging the duties of that situation he continued to reside in his father's house; and was accustomed to walk to his school and back again each day, but to him, with his athletic frame and buoyant step, the twelve miles' walk was but a pleasant exercise. During his connection with the Parish School he enjoyed the privilege of sitting under Mr Lachlan's preaching, and of being admitted by him to the closest private intercourse. How his face used to light up in after years at the remembrance of the sermons and the conversations of those days!

Not long after his licence he attended a communion at Applecross, at which Mr Lachlan was principal assistant. On Saturday Mr Lachlan was appointed to preach a Gaelic sermon in the open air, but such was his state of mind in the morning of that day that he abandoned the idea of preaching and resolved to remain in his bed. He sent for ''John,'' as he always called my father, about breakfast-time, and insisted on his preaching for him. It was not easy to think of taking Mr Lachlan's place, but there was ''no help for it,'' and he was obliged to promise to preach. The advice given him by Mr Lachlan was — ''When you are asked to preach on an hour's notice spend one half of the hour on your knees pleading for a text, a sermon and a blessing, and the other half employ in studying the text and context, and in gathering as many parallel passages as you can find.'' The time for beginning the service arrived, and the preacher went to the meeting place. The tent in which he stood was constructed with oars in the form of a cone, covered with blankets, and having an opening in front, with a board fixed across it, on which the Bible was placed. Unobserved by the preacher, and just as he had begun his sermon, Mr Lachlan, lifting the blanket from the ground at the back of the tent, crept in behind him, and sat down. The sermon had not proceeded far when a case was described which was so exactly Mr Lachlan's at the time that he could not refrain from exclaiming aloud. Starting on hearing the voice from behind, the preacher, not a little disconcerted, looked round, on which Mr Lachlan kindly said to him, "Go on, John, I have got my portion, and my soul needed it, and other poor souls may get theirs before you conclude." Thus encouraged, the preacher proceeded, the Lord was with him, and his sermon was blessed.

About two years after being licenced he was appointed to preach in Lochbroom, the parish minister having been suspended. The time which he spent there was in some respects the happiest portion of his life, and a light rested on it that drew the eye of memory frequently towards it. It was the season of his "first love" as a preacher; the Lord was very near to his soul, and a manifest blessing rested on his labours. During that time many souls were truly converted unto God, some of whom, in Lochbroom, and some in other places, to which they were scattered, continued till their death to shine as "lights in the world." Many a sweet hour of communion with the Lord he enjoyed in those days in the woods of Dundonnell!

I cannot forget a trying scene, into which a streak of the light of those days was once cast to cheer my heart. Being called to see a dying woman, I found on reaching the place to which I was directed a dark filthy attic, in which I could observe nothing till the light I had carried in had quite departed from my eye. The first object I could discern was an old woman crouching on a stone beside a low fire, who, as I afterwards ascertained, was unable to move but "on all fours." Quite near the fire I then saw a bed, on which an older woman still was stretched, who was stone blind, and lying at the very gates of death. The two women were sisters, and miserable indeed they seemed to be; the one with her breast and face devoured by cancer, and the other blind and dying. They were from Lochbroom; and we had spoken but little when one of them referred to the days of my father's labours in their native parish, and told of her first impression of divine things under a sermon which he preached at that time. The doctrine of that sermon was as fresh in her mind, and as cheering, as when she first heard it half-a-century before. Such was the humble hope of both of them, and their cheerful resignation to the will of God, that I could not but regard them, even in their dark and filthy attic, as at the very threshold of glory. I left them with a very different feeling from that with which I first looked on them; nor could I, after leaving them, see among the gay and frivolous whom I passed on the street, any who, with all their health, cheerfulness, and comforts, I would compare in point of true happiness with the two old women in the cheerless attic.

CHAPTER II

IN 1802 he was appointed missionary at Eriboll. It was on a Saturday he first arrived there. The people were looking for the new minister, and were watching the road by which they expected him to come. They saw a young man of a fair complexion and a frame that seemed in their eyes a model of symmetry and power walking past with a step so light that it scarce bent the heather; but the more they admired the athletic Highlander the further were they from conjecturing that he was their future minister. To the no small surprise of the people, the traveller whom they observed on the Saturday mounted the pulpit on the Sabbath, and before the service was over they were all disposed to join with Major Mackay, who said, ''We had a minister before, who was a Christian, but we have now a minister who is both a man and a Christian.'' His text on that Sabbath was Isaiah 40: 11; and, through the sermon preached, several persons received their first impressions of divine things who gave proof till their death of their having in their hearts the true fear of the Lord. On the ministry thus auspiciously begun, the blessing of the Lord rested till its close.

Eriboll had enjoyed the ministry of Mr Robertson, afterwards of Rothesay and of Kingussie, and of Mr M'Bride, afterwards of Arran. The labours of these men of God had been blessed, and the fruit of them appeared in a goodly remnant of living souls, who were the ''light'' and the ''salt'' of the district, and in the respect for the means of grace entertained by the whole body of the people. My father often spoke of a certain glen, in which about thirty families resided, in each of which there was, at least, one who feared the Lord and in each of which there was the true worship of

God. The houses in this blessed hamlet were close together, around the sides of an amphitheatre, through which a small river had torn a course for itself. Standing on the edge of the declivity above this glen on a quiet summer evening, one could hear the songs of praise from all these houses mingling together before they reached the listener's ear, whose heart must have been hard indeed if they failed to melt it. One, at least, did feel while listening to the psalm-singing in these blessed homes, as if the place were none other than the house of God and the very gate of heaven. By one ruthless eviction all the tenants of that glen were banished from their homes, and the most of them found no resting-place till they reached the backwoods of Canada.

Though it was at Eriboll he resided and most frequently officiated, he was required to preach occasionally at Melness, in the parish of Tongue, and at Kinlochbervie, in the parish of Eddrachillis. The distances between these places are considerable, and as there were then no roads, it required no ordinary strength, and it taxed the best pedestrian to overtake the necessary amount of work. Often, while in that charge, has he walked more than twenty miles to the meeting-house, over marsh and moor, and sometimes preached thereafter in clothes quite drenched with rain. But the Lord fitted him for such work, and his constitution came "scaithless" out of it. On one occasion, walking from Eriboll to Rhiconich, he was accompanied by his beadle and by his youngest brother, then a mere boy. They had not proceeded far when a snow-storm came on, and his little brother became quite exhausted. Raising him in his arms, my father carried him, and not only kept up with the beadle, but left him behind. The interval between him and the beadle was increasing so fast that he at last waited till he came up, when he found him so wearied that he was compelled to relieve him of the portmanteau which he carried, and to strap it on his own back. Those who were waiting his arrival at the journey's end were not a little surprised to see him coming with the bag on his back, and the boy in his arms, and dragging the beadle by the hand.

Major Mackay then resided at Eriboll. Faithful in the service of his earthly sovereign, he was, at the same time, "a good soldier of

Jesus Christ.'' It was a rare sight to see him rise on a Communion Friday, in his regimentals, to ''speak to the question.'' A gentleman, a soldier, a Highlander, and a Christian at once, it was no wonder that he was loved and respected, and this might be seen in the eager attention of the people when he rose to address them.

For his daughter, Mrs Scobie of Keoldale, my father always cherished the highest esteem and affection. He corresponded with her during the whole of his life, and his letters to her indicate the warmest Christian friendship. She was generally regarded as the model of a Christian Highland gentlewoman. Her intellect was of a high order. Her appearance and bearing were such as would befit one of the highest stations in society. Many had proved her hospitality, and all of them found her heart fraught with kindness and her pleasant home with comforts. The poor found her charity always fervent and her hand always full. But beyond all these in price were her devotion to the fear of the Lord and her fervent affection for His servants and people.

With Mr Mackay, of Hope, my father was very intimate. He was a man eminent for godliness. The following anecdote, connected with his last days, is given on authority that may not be questioned. My father was to preach on a certain day in a place not far from his house. Mr Mackay, though very ill, would allow none of the family or domestics to remain with him, insisting on all in the house going to hear the sermon. On their return, someone remarked to him that it was a precious sermon they had heard that day. ''Well my soul knows that,'' he said, ''for, though lying here, my mind was following the preacher's, as he was engaged in his work,'' and, to their utter astonishment, he mentioned the text, and repeated much more of the sermon than could those who actually heard it. This story, seemingly so incredible, is perfectly true, and furnishes a most remarkable instance of the mysterious fellowship of the saints.

The godly Donald Macpherson was still alive when my father was in Eriboll, of whom he has often said that, of all the Christians he had ever known, he was the man who lived nearest to the Lord. Many an hour of sweet profitable converse have they spent together. They have been known to retire to a lonely hillside, and there to spend, in prayer and conversation, a long summer day. It was exceedingly sweet to my father to recall the memories of this eminent saint. He was, in some respects, more like a seer of the days of old than the ordinary Christian of the present time. His nearness to God in prayer was remarkable. Seldom did he specially carry one's case before the throne, without its being so laid open to him, that there was scarce a thought or feeling of the party prayed for hidden from him by the Lord. Remarkable instances of this might by multiplied.

The well-known Robert Macleod was Donald Macpherson's devoted disciple. In whatever way Robert was at first awakened, it was through Donald's blessed instruction he was established in "the truth as it is in Jesus," and never was a soul more tenderly and wisely nursed than that of this interesting inquirer. Ardent and honest, he in his outset needed a judicious friend; and in Donald Macpherson he found one who could understand all his peculiarities, and who carried his case so closely under the light from the mercy seat that few of his fears and sorrows were hidden from him. No wonder though he venerated this man of God. The story of his first prayer in Donald's family has been often told. To Robert's bewilderment, his host abruptly asked him to pray at family worship during a visit which he paid him. He dared not refuse, so turning on his knees and addressing his Creator, he said, "Thou knowest that though I have bent my knees to pray to Thee, I am much more under the fear of Donald Macpherson than under the fear of Thyself." Donald allowed him to proceed no further, but tapping him on the shoulder, said, "That will do, Robert; you have honestly begun and you will honourably end," and then he himself concluded the service. Poor Robert's first attempt was not, he himself thought, very encouraging, and he was expressing to his friend his fear that he never could be of any use in bearing a public testimony for the truth. "Yes, Robert," his friend soothingly said, "the Lord will open your mouth to speak the praises of free grace, and as a sign of this, you will be called thrice to speak the very first day you are called to speak in public." Soon thereafter Robert heard that the communion was to be dispensed in Lochbroom, and that

Mr Lachlan was expected to be there. He went on the appointed week, but did not reach the place of meeting at Lochbroom till after the commencement of the service on Friday. He had not arrived when Mr Lachlan was opening the question, and yet, strange to say, the minister declared that he expected a recruit to the ranks of the speakers that day, from whatever quarter he might come. Robert just then made his appearance, and was not long seated when he was called to "speak to the question." He did not refuse to rise, but was so embarrassed as to be able to utter only a few hurried words. Towards the close of the service, and after many others had spoken, Mr Lachlan called Robert again, and said to him, "As you were taken by surprise before, you could not be expected to say much, but rise again, and the liberty formerly denied will be given you." Robert arose and delivered a most affecting address, which so delighted the minister, that he called him to conclude the service with prayer. This was Robert's first public appearance, and he was called thrice to speak; and thus the sign was given to him which Donald Macpherson had led him to expect.

A remarkable instance of Robert's warm love to the brethren, and his nearness to God in prayer, has often been repeated, and is undoubtedly true. The case of the godly John Grant was pressed closely on his spirit, along with an impression of being in temporal want. He was strongly moved to plead with God for "daily bread" for His child, and so constantly was he thinking of him for three days, that at mid-day of the fourth, he resolved to set out for John's house, and he gave himself little rest till he reached it. Full of the impression that stirred him from home, he arrived at the house, and entering it, went at once to the place where the meal-chest used to be, and, to his astonishment, found it nearly full. "This is a strange way, Robert, of coming into a friend's house," John said, as he advanced to salute him. "Were you afraid I had no food to give you if you should remain with me to-night?" "No," was Robert's answer, "but that meal-chest gave me no small trouble for the last few days; but if I had known it was so far from being empty, as I find it is, you had not seen me here to-day." "When did you begin to think of it?" John inquired. Robert mentioned the day and the hour when his anxiety about his friend began. ''Well, Robert,'' John said, ''the meal-chest was then as empty as it could be; for how long were you praying that it might be filled?'' ''For three days and a half I could scarcely think of anything else,'' Robert answered. ''O what a pity,'' his friend said, ''you did not complete the prayers of the fourth day, for on the first I got a boll of meal, another on the second, and a third on the day following, but on the fourth day only half a boll arrived, but now you are come yourself, and I count you better than them all.'' Then rejoicing in each others' love, and in the love of their Father in heaven, who heareth the cry of the needy, they warmly embraced each other.

A still more remarkable person then resided within the bounds of the Eriboll Mission — Miss Margaret M'Diarmid, afterwards Mrs Mackay. She was a native of Perthshire, and came to reside in Sutherland along with a brother. During his lifetime, she was known only as a giddy girl, full of fun, and with a way of doing things quite unlike that of all around her. It was her brother's death that was the means of fixing her attention on eternal things. He had been deer-stalking on a winter day when the lakes were frozen over. Anxious to be at a certain point before the herd of deer, he ventured on a frozen lake that lay between him and his goal. He had not gone far when the ice gave way, and he sunk in a moment and was drowned. The shock to his sister was appalling, but the season of her anguish was the Lord's set ''time of love.'' Her soul's state and danger soon drew her mind from the affliction of her brother's death, and she was the subject of a searching work of conviction when my father came to Eriboll. Under his preaching she was led to the foundation laid in Zion, and her new life began in a flush of fervent love that seemed to know no waning until her dying day. She was one among a thousand. Her brilliant wit, her exuberant spirits, her intense originality of thought and speech and manner, her great faith, and her fervent love, formed a combination but rarely found.

During the summer of each year she was accustomed for a long time to come to Ross-shire, in order to be present on communion seasons, wherever she was sure of hearing the gospel and of meeting the people of the Lord. In all those places her presence was like sunshine, and many a fainting spirit was cheered by her affectionate counsels. Her greatest enjoyment was to meet with anxious inquirers, and many such have cause to remember for ever the wisdom and tenderness of Mrs Mackay's advices.

Her visits sometimes extended to Edinburgh and Glasgow. On one occasion she abruptly announced to her husband her intention of starting for the south. Her purse was at the time almost empty, and her husband could not replenish it; and she was also in a very delicate state of health. All this her husband was careful to bring before her, with a view to dissuading her from attempting the journey she proposed. But, assured that the Lord had called her to go, she would not look at the "lion in the way," and met every reference to her empty purse by saying, "the children ought not to provide for the fathers, but the fathers for the children, and it is not the Father in heaven who will fail to do so." In faith she started, and not a mile had she walked when a gig drew up beside her, and the gentleman who drove it kindly asked her to take a seat. Thanking him in her own warm way, she sprang into the gig, and was carried comfortably all the way to the manse of Killearnan. But it was the smallest part of her journey to Edinburgh that was passed on reaching Killearnan, and she could not calculate on travelling over the rest of it with an empty purse. Her faith, however, failed not, and "the Lord will provide" was her answer to every fear that rose in her heart and to the anxieties expressed to her by others. Hearing that the sacrament of the Supper was to be dispensed at Kirkhill on the following week, she resolved to attend it, and to postpone her visit to the south till after it was over. She went, and on Monday a gentleman made up to her, after the close of the service, who handed to her a sum of money, at the request of a lady who had been moved to offer her the gift. Mrs Mackay gratefully accepted it; but, being accompanied on her way back to Killearnan by a group of worthies, all of whom she knew to be poor, she divided all the money among them, assured that it was for them she received it, and that provision for her journey would be sent by some other hand. Her expectation was realised. A sum fully sufficient was given to her, and she started on her journey to the south.

Travelling by the stage-coach, she was accompanied by several strangers, who were quite struck with her manner, and afterwards fascinated by her conversation. One of them venturing to ask whence she had come, her beautiful and striking answer was, ''I am come from Cape Wrath, and I am bound for the Cape of Good Hope.'' On one account alone they were disposed to quarrel with her. At that time there was a change of drivers at each stage, and at every halt ''remember the coachman'' was called out at the window. Mrs Mackay invariably gave a silver coin and a good advice to each of the drivers. Her companions, not liking to be outdone by their strange fellow-passenger, and liking still less to part so freely with their money, at last remonstrated. ''We cannot afford to give silver always,'' one of them said, ''and we cannot keep pace with you in liberality.'' ''The King's daughter must travel as becomes her rank,'' she said, as she again handed the silver coin and spoke the golden counsel to the driver. Before they parted her companions were persuaded she was the cleverest, and the pleasantest, but the strangest, person they had ever met. Many a refreshing visit she paid to all the Lord's people whom she could reach before she returned home; and when she did, it was with more strength in her frame and more money in her purse than when she left it. Her husband, who had so strongly dissuaded her before, could only wonder now and give thanks to the Lord for His gracious care of her by the way. Of him she used to say, ''he was just made for me by the Lord's own hand; the grace he had not at first has now been given him, and he will allow me to wander for bread to my soul wherever I can find it.''

She was usually called ''the woman of great faith.'' ''The woman of great faith!'' a minister once exclaimed on being introduced to her for the first time. ''No, no,'' she quickly said; ''but the woman of small faith in the great God.''

In repartee few could excel her or tried to get the advantage over her without being foiled in the attempt. On one occasion she met with Mr Stewart of Cromarty, and few ever more dexterously poised a lance or were more skilful of fence than he. He had heard of Mrs Mackay, and resolved to draw her out. His congenial spirit soon evoked all her wit. Getting the advantage over him, Mr S. threw himself on the sofa, exhausted by the excitement of the rencontre and a little chafed under a sense of defeat. A brother minister wished him to sit up and to renew the conversation, which had been so delighting. "Oh! let him alone," Mrs M. said, patting him on the head, "every beast, you know, must be after his kind"; showing how well she had marked his originality, and how skilfully she could feather the arrow of rebuke with a compliment.

Dr Mackenzie, when minister of Clyne, used, as often as he could, to bring his godly uncle to preach on a week day in his church. He invited on such occasions all the ministers of the Presbytery to be his guests at the manse. Mrs Mackay was present on one of these days, and being seated in the drawing-room after the service in church was over, the minister of Tongue came in. Rushing up to him in her own eager way, "Glad I am to see, and still more glad to hear you," she said. "Oh, you could not have been glad in hearing me to-day," Mr M'K. said, with a sigh, "for I had but little to say, and even that little I could only speak in bonds." "Hush, man," was her quick reply,

> "A little that a just man hath
> Is more and better far
> Than is the wealth of many such
> As lewd and wicked are."

And, as she repeated the last two lines, she waved her hand across the group of Moderates who were seated beside her.

Her faith, always remarkable, triumphed in a season of affliction. A beloved son was once drowned before her eyes, quite near the shore, in front of her house. The body was soon found, and the mother, supporting the head of the corpse as they carried it to the house, was singing with a loud voice the praises of the Lord. She had learned, as few Christians have ever done, to show the dark side of her case only to the Lord. However low her hope might be, and however harrowed her feelings, she would allow none to see a tear in her eye, or to hear a groan from her heart, except those with whom her secret was safe, and who would not be discouraged by her distress. Many were thus led to think that her sky was always without a cloud. It was far otherwise under God's eye; but the Christless never saw in her what would prejudice them against a life of godliness, and the godly were always encouraged by her ever-radiant cheerfulness.

Till her last illness her spirits had never sunk, nor had her mind lost aught of its activity and clearness. She died in April, 1841. Even while lying on her death-bed, her cheerfulness did not forsake her, and she was always ready to give a word of advice or encouragement to all who approached her. Her husband had heard, a few days after it had occurred, of my father's death, and determined not to communicate the tidings to his dying wife, as she was so soon to know it by meeting his spirit in the region of the blessed. With this resolution he entered her room and sat gloomily down on a seat by the fire. "I know what ails you," his wife said to him soon after he was seated, "you have heard of Mr Kennedy's death; I knew of it before. He died," she added, "on Sabbath evening, and," mentioning a certain day, "before then I will join him in the Father's house." And so it was. So knit together and so near to God were the spirits of both that less than the death of either would not be hidden from the other.

The sacrament of the Supper was dispensed at Kinlochbervie while he was missionary in the district. The only minister present with him on that occasion was the parish clergyman. The less that would be given him to do, the better pleased would he himself and all others be, and so the whole burden of the service was left upon the missionary. The only available and comfortable room near to the place of meeting was occupied by the ministers. A considerable number of respectable persons had gathered, among whom were Major Mackay of Eriboll, Mr Mackay of Hope, and several others. In a corner of "the meeting-house," there was a square seat into which heather had been packed, and there, covered with their cloaks, the major and some others slept. The minister's house-keeper, having to furnish the gentry with a light as they retired to their sleeping-place, failed to find a candlestick, and, being anxious to save appearances, was in no small ferment. In great perturbation, she came to her master to tell him that the only candlestick she could set before Major Mackay was "a peat with a hole in it." "There was no better candlestick in the stable at Bethlehem," was his only reply to her statement of grievances. He knew well that those about whose comfort Abigail was so anxious were quite content with whatever provision was made for them. A great crowd of people had gathered, and the parcels of provisions which they carried with them were stored behind a screen, formed of a sail hanging from one of the rafters of the meeting-house. Each one came at stated times for his parcel, that he might eat his crust beside a stream on the hill-side. In barns they found accommodation during the night. But the Lord was in the midst of them, and many felt His saving power and saw His glory during that communion season. On Monday, in particular, so much of the Lord's presence was enjoyed by His people that, to many of them, it was the happiest day of their life. When the time for parting came, none had courage to say "farewell" to the minister. They lingered around him, and followed him to the house; and before they separated, he and they sat down together to a refreshment in the open air. That over, they walked together towards an eminence over which the people had to pass. On reaching the summit, they stood around the minister as he prayed and commended them to the care of the Good Shepherd of Israel. He then said to them, as tears ran down his cheeks, "This is pleasant, my dear friends, but it must end; we need not expect unbroken communion, either with each other or with the Lord, till we all reach in safety our home in heaven"; and, without trusting himself to bid them farewell, he turned away from them, and they, each one weeping as he went, took their respective journeys to their homes.

In 1806 he was called to be assistant to Mr William Mackenzie, minister of Assynt. He had been enabled to decide unhesitatingly, and at once, that it was his duty to accept the offered appointment. What his reasons for this decision were, and how the Lord had revealed His mind to him, there are now no means of ascertaining. But the issue proved that the Lord had indeed taken him by the hand to guide him. No sooner did the people become aware of his intention to remove from Eriboll than grief and consternation spread over the district. Donald Macpherson was the only one who sympathised with him, being persuaded that the Lord was calling him away. To the rest, and even to the best of the people, it seemed very unlikely that the Lord, who had not ceased to countenance his labours among them, should take him from them in the very midst of his usefulness. For a time, they would listen to no argument on the subject; they wished to retain their minister; they could not see the Lord's hand in his removal, and, with tears and entreaties, they besought him to reconsider his decision, and still to remain among them. One after another would wait upon him; groups would be watching for him whenever he went abroad; each one whom he met was weeping at the sight of him; and the congregation always now parted in tears. All this was extremely painful to him, but could not move him from his purpose. He knew what the Lord would have him to do, and he was resolved at any cost to follow His leading. At last prayer-meetings were held by the people, and they were brought to ask for direction "from on high"; and, ultimately, they came to a sober and resigned state of mind and feeling. Donald Macpherson's influence greatly contributed to this result. The night before his departure a deputation waited upon him and intimated to him that they could no longer oppose his removal, as they believed it was of the Lord, although it was on that account more painful to their hearts, fearing, as they did, that by their abuse of the Gospel they had sinned it away. All that they now could do, they said, was to cross as often as they could the hills between them and the scene of his future labours. The state of feeling thus indicated by the people must have been gratifying to their minister as it was creditable to themselves.

The actual parting had now come, and rarely has there been a more affecting scene than that through which he had to pass on the day of his departure from Eriboll. His servant remembers it most vividly. Strong men were bathed in tears, women in groups were wailing as he passed, and all watched to get the last look of him as he went out of sight. His servant, who followed him at some distance, hearing the sound of sobbing from behind a wall, went up to the place from which it issued and found Mrs Major Mackay and Mrs Mackay, Skerra, seated there and weeping bitterly. Poor Barbara could not refrain from joining in the chorus of grief. One of the ladies, turning to her, said, "Little cause have you to weep this day; could we follow him as you do we would soon dry our tears." Their pity was reserved that day for those who remained in Eriboll.

Mr William Mackenzie, the minister of Assynt, was almost all a minister ought not to be, yet he continued to occupy his charge till his death. Always accustomed to regard his pastoral work as an unpleasant condition of his drawing his stipend, he reduced it to the smallest possible dimensions, and would not unfrequently be absent without reason and without leave for many weeks from his charge. This was the usual practice in those days of the Moderate stipend-lifters of Sutherland. The visit of one of them to Ross-shire would be an affair of a month's length at the least, and the people never clamoured for his return. The beadle, who was also the parson's ghillie, invariably accompanied the minister on these excursions. In one case the beadle was also the piper of the district, and during his absence with the minister on one of his jaunts a parishioner was asked when he expected the minister to return. "I don't know and I don't care," was his reply; "if he had only left the piper, he might stop away as long as he pleased."

During the latter part of his life "Parson William" was much addicted to drink. This was known to the Presbytery, but could not easily be proved. The people were unwilling to complain and to give evidence against him. The awe of his office was on them in spite of all the irregularity of his life, and as a man and a neighbour he was rather a favourite. Such of them as might have been expected to act differently cherished the hope of his yet seeing the error of his ways; and while they enjoyed the privileges of the Gospel under the ministry of his assistant, they let "Parson William" alone.

There was the least possible intercourse between the parson and his assistant. Consulting him only when absolutely necessary, the assistant carried on the parochial work in his own way, and was generally not interfered with. The parish was extensive and populous, and the church inconveniently situated. It was necessary, therefore, to divide the parish into districts, each with its preaching station, where the minister was expected to officiate in course.

His work in Assynt was early blessed, and was made effectual for good during the whole of his ministry there. Very seldom has so much been done in so short a time in the conversion of sinners and in the edification of the body of Christ as was done during the period of his labours in Assynt. There were then converted unto God many young men who to old age, and in various districts of the Highlands to which they had scattered, bore fruit, to the praise of the Lord and to the good of His Church. Assynt then became a nursery of Gaelic schoolmasters and catechists, who were afterwards transplanted throughout the north and west, and were known as ''trees of righteousness, the planting of the Lord,'' wherever they were placed. Of those who were then ''turned from darkness into light,'' many, both men and women, were eminent for godliness and usefulness; and there was a peculiarity of feeling and of sentiment about them all that made them marked as a class. This was due to the deep impression their early training had left upon their minds.

To these days of power in Assynt were bound the sweetest memories of those who then enjoyed the presence of the Lord. Often in tears have they spoken of them afterwards amidst the dreariness and trials of the way of the wilderness; and from many a broken heart, and in many an hour of sadness, has the remembrance of them wrung the cry, ''Oh! that I were as in months past, as in the days when God preserved me, when His candle shined upon mine head.''

Amidst his happiness and success in his labours in Assynt he had to bear what in some respects was the greatest trial of his life. Among the young men who then began to make a profession of godliness was one, perhaps the most talented of them all. Norman Macleod, known before as a clever, irreverent, forward youth, began all of a sudden to join himself to the people of the Lord. Claiming to have been converted in a way at least unusual, if not miraculous, he all at once started in the course of profession at a stature and with a courage that seemed never to have known a childhood at all. He began at once to prepare for the ministry. But

Norman's ambition to preach outgrew the slow progress of the stated course of preparation, and cutting short his college studies, he separated from the Church and began to found a sect for himself. His power as a speaker was such that he could not fail to make an impression, and he succeeded in Assynt and elsewhere in drawing some of the people after him for a time. His influence over those whom he finally detached from a stated ministry was paramount, and he could carry them after him to almost any extreme. A few of the people in Assynt were drawn into permanent dissent, and but for the influence that was brought to bear in counter-action of his movement, the whole body of the people would have been quite severed from the Church. Some, even of the pious people, were decoyed by him for a season, who escaped from his influence thereafter, and the people remained as a body unbroken. The anxiety and disappointment of this trying season were peculiarly painful to my father, but the Lord was with him to encourage his heart and to strengthen his hands. This discipline, though trying, was profitable. It kept him humble when there was much to elate him; sharpened his discernment, and doubled his watchfulness in his future dealings with professors; and gave him an opportunity of estimating the motives in which divisive courses usually spring.

It was while in Assynt his marriage took place, an event in which he saw at the time, and loved to trace thereafter, the working of the Lord's own hand. Disposed to love him with all the ardour of a first attachment, prepared to reverence as her husband him who had first espoused her to Christ, and with prudence, of which her whole subsequent life was an unvarying proof, his wife was truly ''a good thing'' of the Lord's own giving. His happiness in his marriage was sweetened by the assurance that he would not have to bear the pain of surviving his wife. This anticipation, which he declared at the time, seemed very unlikely to be verified during the years that succeeded, throughout which he continued in the vigour of unbroken health, while his partner often lay at the very gates of death. But ''the secret of the Lord is with them that fear Him,'' and the pleasing anticipation by which the Lord sweetened the enjoyment of his wedded life was in due time realised.

CHAPTER III

THE parish of Killearnan is pleasantly situated along the northern shore of the Beauly Firth. It derives its name, according to tradition, from the grave of "Irenan, a Danish prince, who fell in battle on its confines, where Cairnirenan still exists." It extends five miles along the shore, and stretches back, two miles to the north, till it reaches the brow of the Black Isle, which, because of its covering of furze, bears the Celtic name of Maolbuie.

Quite near to the shore stands Redcastle, which, owing to its traditional history, was so famous as to have covered the whole parish with its name. It was once a stronghold, and was the scene of some rather famous exploits during the wars of the Stuarts as well as in earlier times. Near it Montrose is said to have been encamped when tidings reached him of the death of Charles. An old manuscript in the hands of the minister who preceded my father contained the following lines, said to have been written by Montrose with the point of his sword, on receipt of the intelligence:

> "Great, good, and just, could I but rate
> My griefs and thy so rigid fate,
> I'd weep the world to such a strain,
> As should it deluge o'er again;
> But, since thy loud-tongued blood demands supplies,
> More from Briareus' hands than Argus eyes,
> I'll sing thy obsequies with trumpet sounds,
> And write thy epitaph with blood and wounds."

In former times the whole parish was under the rule of the Mackenzies, and the people, being yet in a state of serfdom, followed their lairds wherever they chose to lead them. This will account for the strenuous opposition to the Whig ministers which distinguished the parishioners of Killearnan till the first half of the eighteenth century had passed.

Mr John M'Arthur, the first Presbyterian minister after the Revolution, was settled in 1719, and he had but a sorry life during his brief ministry at Killearnan. He was succeeded, though perhaps not immediately, by Mr Donald Fraser, the father of Dr Fraser, Kirkhill, who, about the year 1745, was translated to Ferintosh. He declared, before his removal, that he would not leave Killearnan if there was one man, woman, or child in all the parish who would ask him to remain. Besides these, and before 1758, two others, Messrs Robertson and Williamson, were ministers of the parish. In that year Mr David Denoon was inducted. The state of the parish, when he became its minister, is thus described by his son, who succeeded him: "The generosity of the inhabitants were then ignorant in the extreme, and much disaffected towards our civil and ecclesiastical establishments. As a striking instance of this, the following circumstance is mentioned. The late incumbent was settled minister of this parish in 1758; he, eight months thereafter, publicly intimated after sermon his intention of catechising the inhabitants of a particular district on the following Tuesday; but, on going to the house which he has fixed on as the place of meeting, not above three miles from the church, he found a convention of only a few old women. Having never before seen their minister, they appeared much agitated, telling him, however, that he might have saved himself the trouble of coming to their town, as they had no whisky. They retired, one by one, and alarmed the neighbourhood by saying that a strange exciseman had just come to such a house. Since that period," he adds, "the change is striking. The assiduity of the minister, in the discharge of his parochial duties, was attended with much success." "The house of God is now attended with regularity and devotion. They have learned, not indeed the cheerless refinements of modern philosophy, but, in the perusal of the gospel of peace, to find a healing balm to soothe and comfort them under the pressure of all the calamities of life." The good work, begun under the ministry of the elder Mr Denoon, continued to make progress under that of his son. The latter died in 1806.

At the time of my father's induction, there were upwards of 300 Episcopalians in the parish, in whom were found surviving all the changes that had transformed the whole country around them, much of the ignorance of Scotland's old heathenism, much of the superstition of its Popery, and much of the disaffection of its Jacobitism. Apart from these, the people were now regular in their attendance on the means of grace, in the parish church, neighbour-like in their habits, and with a sprinkling among them of the Lord's "peculiar people."

For nearly seven years before my father's settlement, the parish had been vacant, owing to a dispute as to the right of its patronage, between the Crown and the representative of the Cromarty family. In coming to Killearnan at first, he looked forward to the prospect of being minister of Lochbroom, the scene of his first stated labours as a preacher; but instead of a presentation to that parish, he obtained and accepted a gift of the living at Killearnan. After labouring as an ordained missionary in the parish for nearly a year, receiving for his services a small moiety of the vacant stipend, his induction took place in 1813.

During the same year his father's death took place; an event which, owing to the double tie that bound them, he could not but have deeply felt. Sweet to both had been the occasional visits which, since he had begun to preach, he paid to his father; and they were as profitable as they were pleasant. On these occasions he always preached in his native parish. Once, while preaching there on a Sabbath, he said, in a very marked and emphatic way, "There is one now present who, before coming into the meeting, was engaged in bargaining about his cattle, regardless alike of the day and of the eye of the Lord. Thou knowest that I speak the truth, and listen while I declare to thee that if the Lord ever hath mercy on thy soul, thou wilt yet be reduced to seek as alms thy daily bread." The confidence with which this was said was soon and sorely tried, and he passed a sleepless night under the fear that he had spoken unadvisedly. At breakfast next morning in his father's house several neighbouring farmers were present, one of whom said to him as they sat at table, ''How did you know that I was selling my heifers yesterday to the drover?'' ''Did you do so?'' my father quietly asked him. ''I can't deny it,'' was the farmer's answer. Directing on him one of his searching glances, the minister said, ''Remember the warning that was given you, for you will lose either your soul or your substance.'' ''But will you not tell me how you knew it?'' the farmer asked. The only reply to this was in the words of Scripture, ''The secret of the Lord is with them that fear Him.'' Some of those who heard the warning given to him were often applied to for alms by that farmer during the latter years of his life.

On another occasion, in the same place, while warning sinners of their danger in a Christless state, he suddenly paused, and in a subdued and solemn tone said, ''There is a sinner in this place very ripe for destruction who shall this night be suddenly summoned to a judgment seat.'' Next morning the neighbours observed flames issuing from a hut not far from the ''meeting house,'' which was occupied by a woman notorious for immorality, and in which, when they were able to enter, they found but the charred bones of its miserable tenant.

These are indubitable facts, if not they were not recorded here, though perhaps some may sneer as they read them, and others may shake their wise heads over the supposed imprudence of stating them. A little careful thinking on the subject might help one to see that, by means of the written Word, under the guiding hand of His Spirit, the Lord may give intimations of His will in a way very different from the direct inspiration of prophecy, and that ends are served by such communications of His mind that make it far from improbable the Lord may have given them — for thereby His servants are encouraged, their hands are strengthened in their work, and proof is pressed on the consciences of the ungodly that the true Israel of God are a ''people near unto Him.'' And it is to simple and uneducated people, unable to appreciate the standing evidences of the Gospel, we might expect the Lord to give such tokens of His presence with those who preach it. The improbability of such things to the minds of some is owing to their own utter estrangement from the Lord. This is not the only secret, connected with a life of godliness, which is hidden from them. They know not yet some secrets in that life of which it is death to be ignorant. It is not to its occasional accessories merely that they are strangers, but to its very essentials, and yet who so ready as they to pass judgment on every one of its mysteries. It is a strange fact that the only subject of which one can know absolutely nothing, without special teaching from on high, is of all others, the one on which the most benighted of all "the children of darkness" thinks himself qualified to pronounce. The man who would shrink from directing the blacksmith in shoeing his horse, unless he had studied and practised his trade, will, before one lesson has been given him by the Lord, pass judgment off-hand, with all the airs of an adept, on the hidden life of the people, who alone have "the secret of the Lord." There are some, even of the godly, who are strangers to any such intimations of the will of their Father; but, the longer they live, the less disposed will they be to measure, by their own experience, the attainments of others of their brethren.

The church of Killearnan, till within two years of my father's death, was almost as bad as it could be. Built in the form of a cross, with the pulpit at one of the angles, its barn-like roof unceiled, its windows broken, its doors all crazy, its seats ill-arranged, and pervaded by a dim, uncertain light, it was a dismal, dingy-looking place within. But all applications for a new church, or for a sufficient repair of the old, were refused by the heritors. Tradesmen were found to declare that the church was perfectly safe, and whether it was comfortable or not, the heritors did not care, as they never sat in it themselves. Strange to say, the heritor who chiefly opposed the application for a new church, lost soon after, by fire, much more than his share of the expense of erecting it; the carpenter, who declared the old church to be "good and sufficient," was killed while going to purchase the wood required for the trifling repair that was granted; and the lawyer who represented the heritors at the presbytery, when the application for a new church was refused, was unable thereafter to transact any business. These are facts, and no comment on them is to be added; but there were some who regarded them as the echo from providence, of the voice that proclaimeth, ''Touch not mine anointed, and do my prophets no harm.''

His first sermon, as minister of Killearnan, was on the text, ''God forbid that I should glory, save in the cross of our Lord Jesus Christ''; and not more surely was this the text of his first sermon, than it was the rule of all his ministry there. The plan which he had formed of conducting his work, and the measure of regular service which he had allotted to himself at the outset, he was enabled without intermission to follow and to fill up to the very last week of his life. He preached thrice every Sabbath, held a fortnightly meeting on Monday, and delivered a monthly lecture on Thursday. He catechised his people every year, and visited the sick as occasion required or as the Lord might direct him. On Sabbath the church was almost invariably overcrowded, the Monday meetings were well attended and the church would be nearly full on the Thursday of the lecture, although the service was during the day and in a busy country parish. These monthly lectures were specially addressed to the people of God, and often were they signally blessed. These days were known to be feasting times to the heritage of the Lord, and from great distances were they accustomed to gather to share in the provision of Zion. There were also invariably sermons preached on Christmas and on New Year's Day, both these being idle days in the parish; and seldom, if ever, did either of them pass without ''a brand'' being ''plucked from the fire,'' or one of the Lord's people receiving special help and comfort in the old church of Killearnan.

During all his ministry at Killearnan he was accustomed to preach on communion occasions in all the surrounding parishes to which he had access. His journeys often extended to the western shore of the county, to Sutherland in the north and to Badenoch in the south. His soul never wearied of his Master's work and his health was never impaired by all these journeyings and preachings. ''I wish I could enjoy preaching as you do,'' a brother minister once said to him; ''to me it is comparatively a toil.'' ''No wonder,'' he replied, ''though I should enjoy it, for if ever I had foretaste of heaven's own joy on the earth, it was while preaching

Christ crucified to sinners''; ''and never,'' he said on another occasion, ''did I truly preach the Gospel but while I felt that I myself was the greatest sinner in the congregation.'' The mingled labours and joys of these days are now for ever gone by, but the fruit of these labours shall for ever endure, and the fulness of pleasure, of which these joys were a foretaste, is his in the home of the blessed.

Of his domestic life but little must be written. The record of much that is pleasant to his son to remember would be interesting to the few besides. But outwardly and spiritually his was a life of unusual happiness. Death had never visited his family till sent to summon himself to his home. The partner of his temporal lot was one who, by her watchfulness and wisdom, preserved him from many an annoyance that might have fretted his spirit and interfered with his work. His home life was indeed a holy life. Few ever spent more time in secret prayer or more fully evinced that on communion with the Lord their happiness mainly depended. In anything connected with his temporal lot, beyond its bearing on his work and on the welfare of his family, he took no interest whatever. Of all the animals about the manse his favourite pony that bore him on his Gospel errands was the only one he could recognise as his own.

In the eldership in Killearnan during the first years of his ministry there were no ''men of mark.'' There were a few simple-minded praying men who could have no commanding influence over the people, though their lives did not weaken the little which they had. John Dingwall, for many years his precentor, and one of his elders, was a simple, loving being, living peaceably with all men and walking humbly with his God. In his dotage, which extended over the last few years of his life, he read and prayed and sang, and sang and prayed and read, all day long. Every day was then a Sabbath to John and every week a communion season. I have heard him ask a blessing five or six times before he would begin his dinner. So soon as he was reminded of his dinner being before him he at once began to ask a blessing, forgetting that he had done so before, until, at last, it became very doubtful whether the dinner would be eaten at all.

Simon Bisset was, naturally, a very different character. As transparently honest as John, he was far from being so amiable, and had a much more vigorous intellect. Uncompromising in his opposition to all that he did not approve, he was quite as ready to confess his error when convinced that he was wrong. His minister had been the first to introduce a yearly "private communion" — so called because it was especially intended for the benefit of his own congregation alone, and because, being held in winter, not many strangers could be present. Simon was quite opposed to the innovation, because it appeared to him to preclude all strangers from the privileges of the feast, and he declared that he would take nothing to do with the work. He kept his resolution till the Sabbath, but the action sermon of that day quite overcame him, and no sooner were his services required for keeping an open passage to the table of the Lord than he rose to take his place with tears in his eyes. The sermon was on the character of "the good Shepherd." A boy from Contin, just entering on his teens, was standing in the aisle during the former part of the service, his eyes fixed on the preacher, and an expression of earnestness and, at last, of delight on his face. Simon found him in his way as he went to clear out the passage for communicants, and was about to remove the boy, when the minister observed him. "Leave him, Simon," he said, "that may be one of the good Shepherd's lambs." The elder was in such a softened, loving mood that, in presence of all the congregation, he threw his arms around the child, and gently placed him on a seat. That interesting boy gave the brightest evidence afterwards of his being "a lamb of the flock." He had given his heart that day to the Lord, was carried in the arms of the good Shepherd very swiftly over the wilderness way, and within a year he was added to the flock that is led by "the Lamb" to the "fountains of living water" above. The Sabbath service over honest Simon could not rest till he had confessed his fault to the minister. Coming to the manse, he requested an interview, during which he confessed, with tears, how greatly he had erred in opposing the private communion, acknowledged how his soul had been feasted during the day, and declared his resolution never to oppose what the Lord had so manifestly blessed.

There were others in the eldership whose memories are sweet to those who knew them, but of whom nothing can be written that would be interesting to strangers besides what may be recorded of everyone who walks in the fear of the Lord.

Soon after his admission, he began to catechise in the east end of the parish, in a district which, at that time, was a colony of Episcopalians. The Episcopal clergyman himself, either not deigning or fearing to be present, sent his most trusty man to oppose the parish minister, in the event of his making any attack on the doctrines or on the practices of his Church. The champion of prelacy was present all the time, and had to listen to many things that were far from being pleasant, but he had not the courage to cause any interruption of the service. But he became bold, like many a warrior before him, just when the field-day had passed, and, surcharged with revenge, he waited about the door till the minister came out. Getting tongue at last, he began to abuse, in no measured terms, the minister and his doctrine. Listening quietly for a little, and then fixing one of his piercing looks on the man, the minister spoke a word to his conscience, as it was given him at the time, mounted his horse, and was gone. What was spoken to his conscience had reached and pierced it; and but few days passed when the champion of prelacy came to the manse, asking, "What must I do to be saved?" The wound was deepened, till the Lord's hand bound it; and from among the most unpromising of his flock the Lord thus raised up, as a witness for the truth, the most unpromising individual of them all.

Inroads continued to be made on the colony of Episcopalians till, some won by the power of grace, and others drawn by the current of example, only a very few old people were to be found in the parish, at the period of my father's death, who crossed the threshold of the Episcopal Chapel.

After the peace of 1815, soldiers who had been engaged in the Peninsular war returned, as pensioners, to their native parishes. In general, they were no acquisition. Judging of them as they were on their return, Killearnan's share of the pensioners formed no exception to the rule. But some of them had been preserved amidst all the dangers of campaigns and battles, and brought to Killearnan, that the Lord, in "His time of love," might meet with them there.

Alexander Macdonald, "a Waterloo man," came to reside in a village quite close to the church. Addicted to drink, and pestered by a fretful wife, the poor pensioner led but a miserable life. His home was often the scene of unseemly squabbles. This state of matters continued for some time after his return from the Continent. But, at last, the day of his salvation did come. While in church, on an ordinary Sabbath, the Lord applied the doctrine of the sermon with power to his soul. He was quietly but effectually drawn unto Christ by the cords of His love; and he, who entered church that day in all the indifference of a hardened transgressor, left it rejoicing in the Lord. This was a case in which we might have expected a more protracted and painful preliminary work; but the Lord is sovereign and giveth no account of His ways. The pensioner was soon missed by his former companions. Neighbours observed that a calm had settled on his once restless home. He began to attend the prayer and the fellowship meetings, and many were wondering what had befallen the pensioner. They had not heard of any process of conviction of which he had been the subject; they only knew that he was not now what he used to be before. It was with no small wonder, then, that they saw him rise within a few months after this change to propose a question at the fellowship meeting. Still greater became their surprise when, instead of instantly refusing, the minister most gladly accepted it, expressing at the same time, his assurance that it was proposed under the guidance of the Lord. The pensioner had not then spoken to the minister in private, and this being known by the people, their astonishment was all the greater, because of his manner of receiving the question. But the pensioner's case had been on the minister's heart, and the Lord had led him to expect that he would yet be a witness for Himself, and had prepared him to receive him as such. That day's meeting was countenanced by the Lord, and was an occasion of gladness to minister and people.

The pensioner's life from that day forth was a striking evidence of the power of grace. A more temperate man there was not in all the parish. His house was a very model of cleanliness and neatness within and without. His garden was always the neatest, the earliest, and the most productive. His wife continued the impersonation of fretfulness and discontent she ever was before, but never did she draw an angry retort from her husband. Remembering his former unkindness, there was no self-denial he would not practise, no drudgery he would not submit to, no expense he would spare to add to the comfort of his wife. Never was wife more tenderly treated than she now was, and though an approving smile or a grateful word would never be given in exchange for his kindness, the pensioner never wearied in his tender attention to her wants. His was, indeed, the path of the just, and it shone "more and more unto the perfect day." His Christian course was not long, but it was bright. He had his burden, but he found it light; he had his conflict, but it was short; and, leaving behind him the fragrant memory of the righteous, he passed into his rest in heaven.

At a later period Alexander Macleod returned to the parish. He had been in the Grenadier company of his regiment, and a fine-looking soldier he must have been. About six feet in height, he carried himself so erectly since the days of his drilling that, when he had on the long cloak which he usually wore, he seemed gigantic in stature. He is "the long pensioner" in the memories of my boyhood, and that was the name by which he was known in the parish. He had been wounded severely during a siege, and left among the dead when the wounded were carried to the hospital. It was when they came to bury the dead they discovered that Macleod was breathing. When he was brought to the hospital his case seemed so hopeless that the surgeons would bestow no attention on his wound till more promising cases had been treated. At last he was examined, his wound was dressed, and he gradually recovered, till able to avail himself of his discharge, and return to his native land. On the first occasion on which he called to procure the attestation of his schedule in order to the payment of his pension, he walked up proudly to the front door of the manse, and demanded, in a most imperious tone, an audience of the minister. Being admitted to the parlour, he soon began his stories of the war, and so shocked the minister by the profusion of oaths which he mixed up with his narrative that, after rebuking him, he was compelled to leave the room. A year had not passed when one day "the long pensioner" was seen walking with a hesitating step towards the back door of the manse, a greater contrast to his former self than he could be to almost any other. On entering, he anxiously asked the servant if the minister was at home. He was evidently in deep distress; a tremor shook his whole frame, and tears were falling fast from his eyes. His heart had been pierced by the arrow of conviction on the previous Sabbath, and he had now come, in deep agony of spirit, seeking an answer to the question, "What must I do to be saved?" His convictions of sin were deep, but in the Lord's good time "the oil of joy" was given him "for mourning, and the garment of praise for the spirit of heaviness." For a few years only did he live thereafter. He never recovered from the effects of his wound, but as his bodily vigour was yielding before the progress of disease, his soul was advancing in the knowledge of the truth. It was refreshing to those who delighted in the triumphs of grace to see that noble-looking man, now a broken-hearted sinner, listening to the Gospel in tears. Known and trusted as a sincere follower of the Lamb by all the people of God in the parish, he continued to advance in knowledge and in holiness to the end of his life. One morning, while engaged in prayer during family worship, he suddenly stopped, laid himself down on the floor, and without a movement thereafter, he expired.

It is not often that after three score years and ten a sinner is turned "from darkness unto light," and whenever this is done the riches, power, and sovereignty of grace are gloriously displayed. On this account, other interesting cases of conversion are passed over, to make room for a sample of converts from among the aged.

Alexander M'Farquhar remembered '45 quite distinctly. He had seen Prince Charlie, and had heard the guns on the day of Culloden. Often did he tell to wondering groups of listeners his stories of those days, and filling up from his imagination the blanks in his memory, marvellous, indeed, were his tales of Charles and his exploits. The

Prince, of M'Farquhar's tales, was a Goliath in height; his horse could be mounted by ordinary men only by means of a ladder; and never was Eastern king, glittering all over with gold and jewels, one half so splendid in his attire as he, according to M'Farquhar's description, who commanded the clans at Culloden. Only as a retailer of fabulous stories of the rebellion, and as a hardened, ignorant, worldly man was he known till he had passed four score years and ten. But then the Lord broke down the strong entrenchments of the kingdom of darkness in that hardened sinner's soul by the almighty power of His Spirit, and won him, as a child is won, by the beauty and the love of Christ. He had passed into his dotage then, but he had not gone beyond the efficacy of the Lord's own teaching. It was wonderful to hear that man, who had lived for ninety years "without God in the world," now describing, with a child's simplicity, his first impressions of the Saviour's love. It was through the preaching of the Gospel, under which he had sat so long a listless hearer, that the light first broke in on his long-benighted soul and he first "tasted that the Lord is gracious." He lived, thereafter, wondering at the change he felt, and at the grace that produced it, till he went in to join the choir who sing the praises of redeeming love in heaven. His new life was, indeed, a short one, but the light shone upon it, in which all around him saw that he was departing "from hell beneath."

Still older was "Colin of the peats," as the schoolboys called him, before the light of truth dawned on his darkened soul. One of my earliest memories is the visit of old Colin to the school with his little cart of peats. We then thought him to be a century old, and his pony's age was reckoned at almost half its owner's. Up to his hundredth year, he continued a dark earthworm, without a thought about his soul, or one care about his safety. His mind, never vigorous, was then in the weakness of a second childhood; and if there was one on earth that seemed quite beyond the reach of grace, it was old "Colin of the peats." Able yet to walk, he was regularly in church. After a Sabbath, on which he was observed to have a wakeful, earnest expression on his deeply furrowed face, he came to his minister. "I saw a most beautiful one last Sabbath," the old

man said, as he sat down in the study. "Where did you see him?"
he was asked. "In the sermon," was Colin's answer. "What was
his appearance, Colin?" "Oh, he was fairer than the sons of men;
I can't tell what he was like, for he was altogether lovely." His
minister then asked, "What effect had the sight of Him on your
heart?" "Oh, he quite took my heart from me," was Colin's
simple and touching answer. This was all that he, then in his
dotage, could tell about the change through which he passed. But,
thereafter, old Colin thought and spoke of Christ, of whom he had
never thought or spoken before, and he cared now to think and
speak of none and nothing else. The little exercise of intellect now
left in Colin's mind was bathed in Gospel light, and the old man's
broken heart gave forth, with all the freshness of a child's affection,
the savour of the love of Christ. A year of this new life was added to
the century during which he lived "without God in the world,"
and then he quietly "fell asleep."

More marked and evident was the conversion of old Sandy Dallas.
Till he reached his seventieth year, there was not in all the parish a
more worldly and insensate man than he. He regularly came to
church, but he gave not even his ear to the Gospel; for no preacher
and no sermon could keep Sandy awake. Busy, late and early, with
his farm work all the week, and thinking of nothing else, Sabbath
was to him a day of rest, just as he could make it a day of sleep. He
chose to take his nap in his pew in church rather than on his bed at
home, but this was all his concession to the claims of conscience. It
was about six years before my father's death that the long slumber
of his soul was broken. The first indication of a change was his
earnest attention to the Word preached. He, who used to sleep out
the whole service in church, now fixed his eye — and he had but
one — on the preacher, and with rivetted attention, and in tears,
seemed to drink in with eagerness all that was spoken. On leaving
the house of God, he was now observed to choose a retired path to
walk in, apart from the crowd; and, though his house was only
about a mile from the church, hours would pass before he reached
it. The elder of his district, observing this, resolved to follow him,
that he might ascertain how he employed his time by the way. He

could easily conceal himself from Sandy, while only a short interval separated them. He approached him closely enough to hear his voice, as he repeated all he could remember of the sermon, and to notice that when his memory failed him he knelt to pray for help to recollect what he had lost; and that when any note particularly impressed him, he would again kneel to pray, asking now the Lord to preserve it in his memory, and to apply it effectually to his soul. This was, thereafter, his usual practice in retiring from the house of God. In course of the following year, he applied for admission to the table of the Lord, and was cordially received by both the minister and the elders. Among the many who came to look on my father's remains after his death was Sandy Dallas; and, of them all, there was not a more heart-stricken mourner. Grasping convulsively the post of the bed on which the corpse was stretched, all his sobbing voice could utter were the words, "He there, and I here!" He survived his minister a few years, during which he gave ample evidence of his affections being now "set on things above." All he now did about the farm was occasionally to herd the cattle, and even then he passed his time in reading and in prayer and praise; others complaining that the herding was spoiled by the praying, and he himself complaining that the praying was spoiled by the herding. The freshness of his spiritual feeling waned not with his decaying intellect and strength, and, as an humble follower of the Lamb, he passed the remnant of his days on earth.

David Munro, till within two years of his death, was the most notorious drunkard in the parish. Seldom sober, and only so when he could not manage to get drink, he passed a beastly life, till he approached four score years of age. But all this time he was regularly in the house of God. This and his terror of the minister were the only evidences of his not being quite abandoned. His dread of my father had all the power of a passion. There was no effort he would not make to avoid encountering him. But an occasion occurred in which he was under the necessity of meeting him. One of his daughters was about to be married, and her father must, of course, come "to speak to the minister," for such was the stern custom of the parish. He could not avoid meeting the minister on the marriage day, at anyrate, so he resolved to come to speak to him in the manse. He came, but in such a state of fear that it was with difficulty he could mount the stair to the study. He came out of it, after a short interview, bathed in tears. Meeting the minister's wife, he said to her, "Oh, I expected to meet a lion in the study, but I found a lamb"; and, quite overcome by the kindness he had met with, he renewed his weeping. His case had been on her heart before, and on those of other praying people, and her feeling towards him was such that she could not refrain from saying, "Would that the power of grace transformed yourself, David, into a lamb." "Who knows, who knows, but it may," he said, as he hurried off. Not long after he was laid low by sickness, and nothing would satisfy him now but a visit from the minister, whom he so dreaded to meet before. My father went to see him, and his visits were blessed to the poor drunkard. After a deep work of conviction, he was led to the only good foundation of a sinner's hope, and lived long enough to give evidence, which assured the hearts of many who were not easily satisfied, that he was verily "a brand plucked from the fire."

Another case is linked with David's in the memories of those days, just because the convert had been a drunkard also. Returning home on a dark night after preaching in Dingwall, my father heard a moan by the wayside which arrested his attention, and on dismounting he found a poor wretch lying in the ditch, helplessly drunk, and almost strangled. Raising, he supported him, as he led his horse to a house at a little distance. There the poor man lay till he had the drunkard's wretched waking next morning. The story of his rescue was told him next day, and it so wrought upon his mind that he resolved to go to thank the person who had so kindly taken care of him. He could not summon courage to pay his visit till that day had passed. Arriving at the manse of Killearnan a little after mid-day on the Thursday of the monthly lecture, he found that the minister had gone to church, and that there was public worship there that day. He went to the house of God, the Lord met with his soul, and he who had been the means so lately of extending his life on earth was now, besides, the means of leading him into the way of life eternal.

A more interesting case than any yet given must now be added as the last in the sample of converts in Killearnan. Mary Macrae lived in Lochbroom till she was more than fifty years of age. She was regarded by all her acquaintances as a witless creature that could not be trusted, as she herself used afterwards to say, "even with the washing of a pot." The little intellect she had was in a state of utter torpor; nothing moved it into activity. Any attempt to educate her was regarded as quite hopeless. Her life was, indeed, a cheerless waste during her "years of ignorance." Regarded as a simpleton by her neighbours, and as a burden by her relatives, she was a stranger even to the happiness which human kindness gives; and no light or joy from heaven had yet reached her alienated soul. On a Saturday, as she sat by the fire in her bothy in Lochbroom, the idea of going to Killearnan came into her mind. Whence or how it came to her she could not tell, but she found it in her mind, and she could not shake it out. She rose from her seat, threw on her cloak, and started for Killearnan. She had never been there before, although she had often heard it spoken of. The journey was long and lonesome, but she kept on her way, and asking direction as she went on, she at last reached the old church of Killearnan as the people were assembling on the Sabbath morning. Following the people, she entered the church. During the sermon the voice of the Son of God was heard by Mary's quickened soul. She saw His beauty as no child of darkness ever saw it, and with her heart she said, before she left the church that day, "I am the Lord's."

Never, from that day till her death, did Mary return to her former home. Where she had found the Lord there she resolved to cast her lot. But the joy of her espousals was soon rudely broken, and deep, for a season, was the agony of her soul thereafter. I used to know her then as "foolish Mary," and wondered what could move my father to admit her to his study, but the time came when I accounted it one of the highest privileges of my lot that I could admit her to my own. By degrees she was raised out of the depths of her sore distress. Marvellous was the minuteness with which Mary's

case was dealt with by the preacher Sabbath after Sabbath. Every
fear was met, every difficulty solved, that distressed and troubled
her; and she, whom "the wise and prudent" would despise,
seemed the special favourite of heaven among all the children of
Zion who were fed in Killearnan. Her mind was opened up to
understand the truth in a way quite peculiar, and she was led into a
course of humble walking with her God.

Owing to the feebleness of her intellect, she could directly apprehend only a logical statement of the very simplest kind. The truth
was first pictured in an allegory, in her imagination, and then
holding the statement of it before her understanding and its symbol
beside it, she examined and compared them both; able to receive
from the former into her understanding only what was made clear
by the latter, and refusing to receive from the latter into her heart
all that did not accord with the former. Regarding a merely imaginative as necessarily a merely carnal view of spiritual truths, one could
not but be staggered at first before Mary's habits of thought. But
in course of time they would furnish to a wise observer a very
distinct delineation of the proper offices of the various mental
faculties in relation to "the things of God." Being all feeble, each
required to do its utmost in its own peculiar place ere a truth
presented to her mind could reach her heart. Because of this they
could the more easily be seen at work in all her mental processes.
Her imagination was employed in introducing the truth into her
understanding, and this must always be its handmaid work about
"the things of God." It must not convey the truth directly to the
heart; it must only help its passage thither through the understanding. When it assumes a more lordly function the light which it
furnishes cannot be safe nor the feeling which it produces healthful.

Like the sickly child in a family, Mary was all the more closely
and tenderly dealt with owing to her very feebleness. Her
imagination could not form the emblem required to assist her
understanding, and the illustrations she employed seemed to have
been the Lord's own suggestions. She could not read, and in her
feeble memory but little Bible truth was stored. The Word seemed,
on that account, to have been directly given her by her heavenly

Teacher. As she could not repair to her Bible to search for it, her daily bread for her soul came to her like the manna, always fresh from heaven, right down upon her case. Peculiarly near was thus her intercourse with God, just because of her very weakness.

Her way of telling any of her views or feelings would be quite startling to a listener at first. It was always easier for her to give the matter as she found it in the emblem than embodied in a formal statement. She seemed, on that account, to one who knew her not, to be telling of some dream or vision she had seen. It was only after she had told the allegory that she could attempt to state what it was intended to illustrate. The emblem was not constructed by her to make her meaning clear to another; it was presented to her by the Lord to make a truth clear to herself. She always felt that it was something given to her, and it was always as vivid as a scene before her eyes. She could not dispense with it, either in examining what she sought to know or in describing what she sought to tell. Meeting a young man once, who was on the eve of licence, and much cast down in prospect of the work before him, she said, "I saw you lately in a quagmire, with a fishing-rod in your hand, and you and it were sinking together, and you cried, as if you would never rise again; but I saw you again, on the bank of a broad river, and the joy of your heart was in the smile on your face, and you were returning home with your rod on your shoulder, and a basket full of fish in your hand;" and then, in broken words, she spoke of his present fears, and of the joy awaiting him in the future.

Of all I ever knew, she was the one who seemed to enjoy the greatest nearness to God in prayer. The whole case of one, whom she carried on her spirit before the throne of grace, seemed to be uncovered before her. She could follow him with the closest sympathy in his cares and sorrows during his course through life, with no information regarding him but such as was given her in her intercourse with God. A minister, to whom she was attached, having been sorely tempted during the week, and finding no relief on Sabbath morning, resolved not to go out to church at all that day. About an hour before the time for beginning public worship, Mary arrived at his house. As she came to the door, he was seated in a room just beside it, and overheard a conversation between Mary and the person who admitted her. "What is the matter with the minister?" she asked. "I don't know," was the reply; "but I never saw him in greater distress." "I knew that," Mary said, "and he is tempted not to go out to church to-day, but he will go after all; the snare will be broken, and he will get on the wing in his work to-day." She then repeated a passage of Scripture, which was "a word in season" to him, who listened out of sight, and a staff to help him on his way to "the gates of Zion."

It was quite extraordinary how her mind would be led to take an interest in the cause of Christ, in places and in countries of which she knew not even the names. Instances of this might be given so remarkable that I cannot venture to risk my credibility by recording them. One only will be given. Coming to me once, with an anxious expression on her face, she asked if there was a minister in a certain district, which she could only indicate by telling that it was not far from a place of which she knew the name. I told her there was; "but why do you wish to know?" I asked. "I saw him lately," was the answer, "fixing a wing to each of his sides, and rising on these wings into the air till he was very high; and then, suddenly, he fell, and was dashed to pieces on the ground;" and, she added, "I think if there is such a minister, that he has but a borrowed godliness, and that his end is near." There was just such a minister, and his end was near, for, before a week had passed, I received the tidings of his death.

Symptoms of cancer in her breast having appeared, and medical advice having been taken, she was told that nothing could be done for her but the removal of the affected part. She was then about sixty years of age, and it seemed to all her friends that she would be running a great risk by submitting to the operation. But Mary had asked counsel of Him to whom she went with all her cares, and, with an assurance of recovery, she resolved to have the cancerous tumour removed. The operation was performed. A few days thereafter she was in the Burn of Ferintosh hearing the Gospel, and never suffered again from the same cause till her death.

Sweet to all who knew her and who saw in her the working of the grace of God is the memory of that simple, loving, holy woman. She is now at her rest in her Father's house; and those who loved her best cannot wish that she still were here. But since she has passed from the earth they often sadly miss the cheering streak of light her presence used to cast across their dark and lonesome path in this vale of tears.

CHAPTER IV

DURING all his ministry at Killearnan, many from surrounding parishes were among his stated hearers. These were a precious accession, for many of them were praying people, and were athirst for the Gospel. Some had received their first impressions of the truth through his preaching, and the strong tie thus formed bound them to his ministry; and others of them found his doctrine to be suited to their cases and resolved to attend where "a word in season" was spoken. A few regularly walked about twenty miles each Sabbath to Killearnan.

To one, at least, the Sabbath journey was nearly thirty miles, for she came from the confines of Sutherland. Leaving home about midnight on Saturday, she walked across the hills regularly in summer and often in winter, and generally without any companion by the way. After the service on Sabbath she returned to her home, and was ready to join in the labour of the farm next morning. On that condition alone would her father allow her to come to Killearnan, being more anxious about the state of his croft than about the salvation of himself and of his family. It was surely owing to "the tender mercies" of the Lord that "worthy Jane Bain" was so long enabled to bear all this fatigue and exposure. Her soul thriving under the Gospel and her body kept from harm, she continued to grow in grace, till, dying in peace, she was removed to the land whose inhabitants toil and suffer no more.

The parish next to Killearnan, on the east, is Knockbain. Mr Roderick Mackenzie, better known as "Parson Rory," was its minister at the time of my father's induction, and for more than twenty years thereafter. More ambitious of being popular as a "country gentleman" than of being acceptable as a Gospel minister, he courted the favour and society of the lairds rather than the love and the fellowship of the saints. Naturally amiable, and impulsively generous, few could apply to him in vain for relief, unless they were deserters of his ministry. For these there was no avenue to his heart. Almost all in Knockbain who desired "the sincere milk of the word" attended on Sabbath at Killearnan. These were all known to "Parson Rory," and their names were on the black list in his books. For the preacher who drew them away he had no liking, and he was not careful to conceal that he had not; and no opportunity of appearing in the pulpit of Knockbain would be given to the minister of Killearnan.

A family resided not far from the manse of Knockbain, whose house was always open to the servants of the Lord. My father often spent a night in this house. His kind host, Mr Munro, would of course ask him to conduct family worship. He could not be punished for doing so, nor could the minister for agreeing to his request. The house of Munlochy was able to accommodate many more than the members of the family, and it would have been very uncivil to exclude any of their neighbours who chose to attend. The barn was still larger, and to it, when the house could not hold them, the family and their friends were, on such occasions, in the habit of adjourning. Often had the barn been repaired to by others when large parties had gathered for a feast and a dance, and they could scarcely be charged with a trespass who used it for the worship of God. No law could be found forbidding the minister to lecture on the chapter which he read, even though the lecture should be quite as long as a sermon, and not very unlike one. In this way a safe opening was found for preaching the Gospel at Knockbain, for which not a few shall for ever give praise to the Lord.

Returning on one occasion from Cromarty, he was prompted to remain all night in Mr Munro's house, but, anxious to be at home, he resisted the suggestion and drove on. He had not got many yards past the crossing when his conveyance broke down, and he was compelled to turn down to Munlochy. The people, informed of his arrival, gathered in the evening to worship. Among his hearers was a youth who amused himself a little before with caricaturing ''the cronies,'' as he called the good people who were coming to the house. In all the levity of wanton indifference he entered the room in which worship was conducted. Soon after the lecture began a case, which he could not fail to recognise as his own, was described, and with such minuteness and authority that the stricken youth imagined every eye in the room was upon him. To his surprise, on looking up, he saw that the eyes of the minister were closed, and that he was quite unobserved by all around him in the room. He then felt that the eye of the Lord alone was upon him, and that the words which were spoken were sent from on high. During a season of sifting temptation which followed, tenderly and wisely was he treated by him through whom the Lord first spoke to his soul; and deep thereafter was their mutual love. I will not in this connection give his name; but I cannot forget that he was the best friend on earth of my soul in the day of my distress. To the end of his wilderness journey may ''the good Shepherd'' preserve and guide him.

Among those who came to Killearnan from Knockbain was a young man whose case was peculiarly interesting. John Gilmour, while a tradesman in Aberdeen, was awakened under the preaching of Mr Grant, then minister of the Gaelic Chapel in that city. His convictions were unusually deep and protracted, and, being utterly unfitted for any active employment, he was compelled to return to his native parish. For several years he walked on the very borders of despair. It was in the study of the old manse of Killearnan the light of the Gospel first shone into his soul. He had come to speak to the minister, but could only tell him of the misery of a soul lying ''without hope'' on the very brink of destruction. In course of conversation, and to illustrate the state of his soul in relation to the Gospel, the minister rose and closed the shutters of the window. When the room was thus darkened he said, ''Such is the state of your soul, John; this room is dark, not because it is not daytime without, and the light not ready to enter, but because the light that shineth so brightly upon it is excluded by something within. It is so with you in relation to Him who is 'the light of the world.''' Then, while gradually opening the shutters, he preached Christ to his disconsolate hearer, and just as the light of day was entering into and filling the room, the "marvellous light" of the Gospel was penetrating into the broken heart of John Gilmour, till the desperate misery of that heart gave place to an ecstacy of joy. The liberty then attained continued with but little intermission till he died; but so overpowering was his gladness that he himself declared his bodily strength was more reduced by three weeks of his happiness than by three years of the misery which he had previously endured. Rapidly growing in grace, and distinguished for the clearness of his views, as well as for the depth of his experience, he seemed one eminently fitted for serving the Lord in the Church on earth. But while yet in his youth he was suddenly removed to his place in the Church in heaven. On Sabbath after his death, my father's text was Psalm 46: 10. Having announced it, he said, "I have searched the Bible throughout for a reason why the Lord should suddenly, and, as we would think, prematurely remove out of the Church on earth one who had given rich promise of usefulness there, but the Lord gave me no account of this dealing, and has only answered my inquiries in the words: 'Be still, and know that I am God.'"

Urray is the next parish on the west, and its eastern boundary is not more than a mile from the Parish Church of Killearnan. A considerable number, from the eastern district of that parish, came statedly to Killearnan on Sabbath. Among them were two, who came always together while they lived, "blind Nelly," and her guide and companion, "old Nanny." Nelly was a lively Christian, with clear views of the truth, and a deep experience of its power. With more than ordinary cheerfulness were combined in her much solemnnity and courage. Living near to the Lord, and having more than ordinary prudence, she and her minister were on very intimate terms, and she was one of those whose visits to the study were always specially welcome. Returning from Killearnan on a Sabbath evening, Rory Phadrig, having missed Nelly from her usual seat in church, called at her house to ascertain why she was absent. Standing before the window of her room, he overheard her voice in prayer, "I cannot be silent," he heard her saying to the Lord, "till

I know why I was kept from Killearnan, for Thou knowest my soul used to be fed there, and that it greatly needed a diet to-day.'' Rory at once removed, and, unwilling to disturb her, went on his way, and, as he himself said, covered with shame, by this proof of her earnestness and boldness, in pleading with the Lord. Rory having on another occasion gone to Nelly's little bothy, along with a friend, so soon as she was aware of their presence, she said: ''I was sure the Lord was going to send two of His people to me to-day, who needed food, for meat for three was sent to me this morning by one who never assisted me before.'' Then, groping her way to her chest, she produced the food which had been so seasonably provided. When death came to ''blind Nelly,'' it found in her a body that old age had ripened for the grave, and a soul that grace had ripened for glory.

Among those who came from Urray was a woman very well known for her kindness to the poor, and for her love to the people of the Lord. Her husband was a farmer in comfortable circumstances, but he did not share in the fervent charity of his wife. Anxious on one occasion to show kindness to a few Christian friends, whom she knew to be poor, she resolved before the Lord to slaughter the best heifer on the farm, and to divide it among them. On announcing her project to her husband, he laughed at a proposal that seemed to him so outrageous, and decidedly refused to allow her to carry her plan into effect. ''I have given the heifer to the Lord,'' she said, ''and if He comes to claim it for the poor of His people, you cannot withhold it.'' On entering the byre next morning, the farmer was not a little astonished to find his favourite heifer lying in the stall, and gasping its last breath. There was now no alternative but to bleed and to flay it, and he was too thoroughly frightened to prevent his wife from disposing, as she pleased, of the carcase.

Shortly before her death, this godly woman was sorely tempted to fear that all her love had terminated in His people, and that none of it had risen up to the Lord Himself. Under the pressure of this temptation she came to Killearnan on the Monday of a fellowship meeting, and called at the manse after the service in the church was concluded. She told her fear to the minister. As she could not doubt her love to the people of the Lord, and as it was proved to her that it was as the brethren of Christ she loved them, he reminded her of the words, ''We know that we have passed from death to life, because we love the brethren.'' As there was no simpler, he assured her there was no surer evidence of grace than that there given; and after explaining to her why she was more conscious of her love to His people than of her love to the Lord, he declared to her, on Scripture warrant, his assurance of the safety of her state in prospect of eternity. His words were blessed to her soul, and she was entirely delivered from her distress. ''There is nothing now left for me to do on earth but to die,'' were her words as she bade the minister farewell; and on the second day thereafter she died.

There were a few from Kilmorack, and after Dr Bayne's death, from Kiltarlity, who statedly waited on his ministry. One of these had received his first impressions of the truth in rather remarkable circumstances. For several years my father occasionally preached in Strathglass, a district peopled chiefly by Papists. Preaching on one occasion beside the river that flows through that lovely glen, a Papist, who dared not to join the congregation, but could not restrain his anxiety to hear, crouched in the thick brushwood that covered the slope of the opposite bank. While lying there, and quite able to hear the words of the preacher, the truth was applied by the Spirit to his soul. He lived to give satisfying evidence to all who knew him that on that day he had begun to ''know the grace of God in truth.''

A reminiscence of another of the hearers from the west is connected with the circumstances of his death. Having attended at Contin on a Communion Sabbath, when my father officiated, after all the other communicants had taken their places at the table, he, for some reason which he did not live to reveal, still remained in his seat. The minister said, ''There is still some communicant here who has not come forward, and till that person take a seat at the table I cannot proceed with the service.'' Another verse was then sung, but ''the merchant from Kiltarlity'' did not come. He was not in the minister's eye, though there was someone on his spirit, when he said, ''I implore you to come forward, for this is your last opportunity of showing forth the Lord's death till He come, for, if I am not greatly mistaken, you will not reach your home in life after the close of this service.'' The merchant then came forward, and no sooner had he taken his seat at the table than the minister said, ''We may now proceed with the service.'' On the dismissal of the congregation on Monday, the merchant set his face on his home, but while crossing the ford of the Orrin he was carried down by the stream and was drowned.

Among those who came from the west was one of whom those who knew her used to say that she was twice married in the same hour. During an excursion to the west, my father preached in Strathbran, which, though now a waste wilderness almost throughout, then contained a considerable population. A marriage party arrived before the hour appointed for preaching, and having a considerable distance to travel to their home, were anxious to start immediately after the ceremony. The minister agreed to marry them at once. During his address, while commending the love of Christ, and presenting first of all, His offer of marriage to each of the parties, the Lord applied the word with power to the heart of the bride, and, before the marriage ceremony was over, she gave herself to the Lord. No persuasion could now induce her to leave the place till the sermon was over. Christ was now the supreme object of her love, and she would not lose the opportunity of hearing His praise. During the remainder of her life she gave satisfying evidence of her having truly known ''the love of Christ that passeth knowledge.''

A few from Dingwall regularly attended at Killearnan on Sabbath. One of these was Kenneth Mackenzie, commonly called ''the Penny Smith.'' He was one of the few who succeeded in keeping their original shape under all the pressure of conventional usage, refusing to take the form and fashion of those who surround them. In his dress, manner, habits, and modes of thinking, he retained his own peculiarity, and would be neighbour-like in nothing. In his kilt and antique coat he seemed to have just stepped out of the midst of the generation of the Fathers. While his neighbours were engaged in idle gossip, or lounging idly by the fire, he was pouring over an old Latin book, spelling through a Hebrew grammar, or writing in characters of his own devising some of his strange thoughts in a record. On the Saturday afternoon his smithy was cleared of its iron and its tools, and seated with benches, on which, for an hour in the evening sat the young men of the neighbourhood, while the smith gave them lessons in psalmody. Not fearing the face of man, it cost him no effort to administer a reproof, whatever the character, rank, and influence of the transgressor might be. Meeting the Sheriff on his Sabbath evening walk, "Lawmakers should not be law-breakers," the smith said to him, as he looked him boldly in the face. "My health requires that I should take a walk, Kenneth," the Sheriff said by way of excuse. "Keep you God's commandment, and you can trust Him with the keeping of your health," was the smith's reply; "accursed must be the health that is preserved by trampling on the law of God."

Hector Maclean was another of the hearers from Dingwall. "Little Hector" he was usually called, for he was not four inches above five feet in height. In his youth he had been engaged in smuggling, as in those days was too commonly the habit. Having lost, by a seizure, the produce of a small quantity of barley, which he had purchased on credit, he was not able to pay for it. Determined even then, to owe no man anything, he accepted of the bounty that was offered for a substitute by one who was balloted for the army; and the sum that was given to him just covered the price of the barley. Soon after joining his regiment, he was sent to Spain with the Army under Sir John Moore. He went through all the adventures of the memorable retreat that terminated in the battle and victory of Corunna. Of all his regiment there were only seven who, on landing in Britain, were healthy and unwounded, and Hector was one of them. Often did he look back on this fact with gratitude and wonder, after he had learned to acknowledge the goodness of the Lord.

Returning to Dingwall after the peace, he resided there till his death. Not long after his return, as he was dressing himself on a morning early in August, he was seized with an unaccountable desire to go to Cromarty. He had never been there before, and was conscious of no inducement to visit it, but he could not repress the feeling that had so suddenly seized him. He started on the journey not knowing whither or wherefore he went. Reaching Cromarty before noon, he followed groups of people who were gathering to an eminence above the town. It was the Saturday of a communion season there. My father preached outside in Gaelic, and Hector was a hearer. The doctrine preached that day the Lord applied with power to his heart, and before the sermon was over he had given himself to the Lord. Few lives were more unblemished than Hector's from that day till his death, few witnesses for Christ more faithful than he, and in simplicity and godly sincerity but very few Christians could excel him.

These are but a few specimens of those who usually came to Killearnan on Sabbath. Almost all of them are now removed from the earth. They no longer require the wells in the valley of Baca, for Zion has been reached, where the Lamb is leading them to living fountains of water, and where they hunger and thirst no more.

During the first half of his ministry at Killearnan, the sacrament of the Lord's Supper was dispensed only once a year, and generally on the first Sabbath of August. Great crowds were accustomed to assemble on such occasions. As many as 10,000 people have met on a communion Sabbath, and nearly 2000 communicants have sat at the table of the Lord. These large assemblies were, of course, in the open air. The place of meeting was a large quarry not far from the church. In front of the rock, which, with the strata of earth that covered it, rose to a height of about a hundred feet, and between two mounds of the rubbish that had been removed during the process of excavation, the minister's tent was erected. There was level ground in front of it, on which the communion tables were placed, and on either side, tier above tier, rose the vast multitude of people. All were able to hear the voice of the preacher, and even its echo from the rock. Sometimes a few adventurous people sat just on the edge of the precipice; but if the preacher was prone to be nervous it was not safe for him to look up to the group on the gallery of the church in the quarry.

An unreasonable prejudice exists in the minds of strangers against the great sacramental gatherings of the Highlands. They are associated in their views with endless confusion and many positive evils. It cannot be denied that, where such large crowds assemble, there will necessarily be much in the outward behaviour of some that is offensive to those who are impressed by the solemnity of the occasion. But of what congregation may not this, to some extent, be affirmed? There was more of this, however, in the days when these gatherings were most honoured by the presence of the Lord than now, when ''the Hope of Israel'' is ''as a stranger'' in the midst of them. When the Lord was doing a great work Satan was busy too. While souls were born again, and the quickened were refreshed, the enemy took his revenge by doing what he could, through the conduct of the openly ungodly, to grieve the hearts of the servants and people of the Lord. But would not that work of the enemy have been got rid of at too great an expense if removed at the cost of losing that work of the Lord? At present much less will be seen in the outward demeanour of a Highland congregation in the open air to offend right feeling than in that of some congregations in the fine temples of the south that may be held up as models of propriety.

It has also been objected that these frequent gatherings must encourage habits of indolence among the people, as they draw them so often away from their stated employments. That they have by some been thus abused cannot be denied. But let it not be forgotten that many of the people in the Highlands had no stated employment and no family to provide for, and were, therefore, free to search for ''the bread of life'' wherever they could find it.

They have been condemned, too, on the ground of their necessarily causing a vacancy in surrounding parishes, whose ministers must be present to assist where the sacrament is dispensed. But if the people attend there, what reason is there for their ministers remaining at home? They could only preach to their own people by leaving their own parishes on that day; and as it must not be supposed that there is any particular virtue in their own pulpits, they may be quite as useful to their people by preaching to them elsewhere. This takes for granted, what was usually the case in days past, that neighbouring ministers would find the whole body of their people in the great congregation before them.

There were two great advantages attending these "public communions," as they were called. An opportunity of fellowship was given by them to Christians from all parts of the country, who would not else have met or known each other on the earth; and the Gospel was preached to a great multitude of sinners by a variety of ministers, amidst the prayers of a great many of God's people. In other circumstances a narrow congregational feeling is apt to cramp the sympathies, even of Christians. Even in the same town, how few are the opportunities of worshipping together afforded to the people of several congregations; and any opportunity of sitting together at the Lord's Table they have not during all their life on earth. The effect of this is, that each congregation becomes a detached self-contained sort of community, with a minister better than every other minister in the town, and who must be extolled at the expense of all others around him. One congregation says, "I am of Paul," and another says, "I am of Apollos," and jealousies arise, causing alienation, where there should be a community of interest and feelings. In widely scattered communities, such as are in the Highlands, there was all the more need of a prevention of this evil. There was, in the wide north, a great tendency to rally round a Paul and an Apollos, and there were some there too — and in all ages they were the worst — who were prone to say, in a spirit of proud exclusiveness, "I am of Christ." But the opportunity which was afforded, on a communion occasion, of hearing all the good ministers of the district, the proofs given of the Lord's presence with each of them, the effect of a community of profit and enjoyment under their preaching, and the loving fellowship of such seasons, tended in a great degree to bring all these sections more closely together and to expand their sympathies and hopes.

On these accounts, while desiring to have the sacrament of the Supper administered also more privately, my father resolved to continue the public communion once a year. Feeling the desirableness of having it oftener than once, and it being impossible to find two days, with a sufficient interval, on which the people could comfortably assemble in the open air; and, anxious besides to be rid of the distractions that necessarily attend the public communion, he resolved to dispense the sacrament of the Lord's Supper in winter. At that season a large number of strangers could not attend, and could not be accommodated even if they did; and it was called, on that account, "the private communion." A strong prejudice against it generally prevailed at first. It looked to some like an attempt to shut out strangers from the privileges of the sacred feast, and to those who viewed it thus it wore a most unchristian aspect. Forgetting that it was only added to the other mode of celebrating the ordinance, they opposed it as if it were its substitute. Some ministers, yielding to the unreasonable prejudice of their people, refused to adopt it; but, in course of time, the feeling against the private communion wore away, and what was at first a solitary and disliked exception became afterwards the rule.

The same ministers for many years invariably assisted in conducting the services of the communion season at Killearnan. He himself usually preached on the Fast-day, alternately in English and Gaelic, choosing always for that day a different language from that in which he preached on Sabbath. His brother, the minister of Logie, always officiated in either language in the action service. There were always some to whom his presence and preaching were peculiarly acceptable. Himself often touching the two extremes of experience, there were a few to whose depths of distress his was the hand to let down the cord that helped them to rise up to light and liberty in Christ. Peculiarly searching and solemn, while sympathetic and clear, his manner quiet, and his style unadorned and simple, there were few who felt attractiveness in his preaching but such as relished the savour of its spirituality. His appearance was very pleasing, and an air of meekness and dignity rested on his countenance, well befitting his position and his work. If there were others his superiors in pleading with men, there was none to excel him as a wrestler with God.

The late Mr Fraser of Kirkhill was always one of his assistants while he lived, and by none was he more loved and appreciated than by my father. His sermons, always remarkable for lucid arrangement, cogent reasoning, and vivid illustration, were peculiarly so in Killearnan. Generally on Saturday he preached in Gaelic on some subject bearing on the priesthood of Christ; and on Monday in English, on the life, privileges, duties, or prospects of believers. These latter were always peculiarly acceptable to the people of God, and oftener than once they were blessed for the conversion of sinners. Mr Fraser's sudden death, which occurred a few years before his own, deeply affected my father. The tidings reached Killearnan after he had gone out to church on the day of the monthly lecture. To the surprise of all, he expressed, in public prayer that day, his persuasion that a breach had been made in the walls of Zion in the north by the removal of one of the eminent servants of the Lord. On coming out of church, and being informed of Mr Fraser's death, he said, "I was prepared for this."

Dr Macdonald was invariably there. He usually preached on Saturday in English, and on Monday in Gaelic. His share of the work was always heartily given, and always heartily relished; and the communion season at Killearnan used to be to himself a time of peculiar enjoyment.

Another of his most able assistants was Mr Sage, of Resolis. Comparatively young, and always given to seeking a lower place than would be assigned to him by his brethren, his portion of the work was usually as small as he could contrive to make it. He contributed his share as if he might be ashamed to present it; but he himself was the only one who wished it were omitted. Yet among us, a representative of other and better days, may the evening of his life be brightened by the light of his Father's face, and may a rich blessing from on high rest on his last works in the vineyard.

What a goodly company of the Lord's people were wont in the earlier days of his ministry to meet at the communion in Killearnan! Many pious men and women from Sutherland, the flower of the worthies of Ross-shire, the most eminent Christians in Inverness-shire, and not a few from greater distances, would meet together there. How precious were the loving fellowships and the wrestling prayers of these saints, and how many proofs were given ere they parted that the Lord was in very deed in their midst!

On Friday the difficulty in these days would be to select, and not as now to find, "men," so many would be present who were qualified to speak, and who would be acceptable to their hearers. Each one who was called to speak knowing this, and unwilling to occupy the time of another, was invariably concise. Hugh Buie would be the first speaker, and clear, full-fraught with thought, and unctuous his remarks would be. Alexander Vass, himself in tears as he spoke of the love of Christ, would move all others to tears by his melting words. Hector Holme, less remarkable than these as a speaker, would be listened to as a man of God, and the unction of his utterances would be sweet to many hearts. John Finlayson, with an experience of the power of the Gospel deeper than his knowledge of its doctrines was clear, would speak a word in season to the simple, broken-hearted Christian. John Gordon would catch the attention of his hearers by some striking allegory, and would be sure to leave some saying in their memories. Donald Fraser would carefully dissect the question, and bring it closely home to the conscience. When Alexander Hutcheson spoke it was as if the alabaster box of ointment was broken in the midst of the assembly. John Clark, with a grace and dignity of manner quite remarkable, would command the respectful attention of all who heard him. In a few broken but savoury sentences Daniel Bremner would follow him. When Angus Ross rose all were eager to listen. A few searching sentences of rebuke addressed to the hypocrite would be followed by a few sweet words of comfort to ''the poor in spirit,'' and he would be soon on his seat again. John Fraser, unconscious of his gift, spoke with peculiar precision and fluency. Roderick Mackenzie, in spite of his rude manner and rough voice, would have earnest listeners, for all knew his thorough integrity, and many felt the point and unction of his remarks. John Munro would speak deliberately, clearly, and to the point. Angus Munro's untutored genius would prove its power in presenting in bold striking words a view of the subject not seen by any other till suggested by himself, and even then appreciated only by a few owing to the intensely metaphysical cast of his thinking. David Ross would always have something to say, at once fresh and striking. And John Macdonald would determine the state of the question with marvellous precision, and would apply it with rare skill. These and some others would have spoken to the question in these days.

Of all these, the two whom my father most fervently loved were Alexander Hutcheson and Angus Ross. Of them he used to say, that of all the Christians he had ever known, except Donald Macpherson, they lived nearest to the Lord.

Alexander Hutcheson was catechist in Kiltarlity during Dr Bayne's ministry there, and thereafter till the infirmities of old age no longer permitted his engaging in his work. He was but eleven years of age when he first felt the impression of the truth. Engaged in tending his father's sheep, one night, as he was shutting them up in the fold, he was strongly moved to kneel down and pray. There, in the midst of his little flock, he fell on his knees, and ere he rose he thought that Christ had won his heart. The impression then made gradually wore away, till he had fallen back into the lethargy that preceded it. Just a year had elapsed, when the same feeling was again excited, and in the same circumstances as before. This, once more, in the course of time wore away. The listlessness which succeeded continued till, one night, just after he lay down in bed, an impression of his guilt and danger as a sinner was made with irresistible power on his heart. So sudden and so overpowering was the awe that came upon his spirit, that he had sprung out of bed, to rush out to the hill, when, as suddenly, the light of the glorious gospel illuminated his soul. Never from that hour did Alexander Hutcheson return to the ways of sin, and thus began his Christian life. Enjoying unwonted nearness to God, he was at the same time a most humble, loving, tender-hearted Christian. It was a fine sight to see him, in his old age, when he rose to speak to the question, as he leant on someone for support, while tears gushed from his eyes at every reference to the love of Jesus.

Angus Ross, more talented than Alexander Hutcheson, was also much more impulsive. The first sermon he ever heard my father preach proved to him peculiarly seasonable. Living in a district once highly favoured but then again a desert, he was just on the eve of seceding from the Establishment. He had gone so far as to be quite ready to join the Secession Church on the very next Sabbath. Hearing that a stranger, who was well reported of, was to preach in a neighbouring parish church, he went to hear him. The text was, "If thou know not, O thou fairest among women, go thy way forth by the footsteps of the flock, and feed thy kids beside the shepherd's tents." During the discourse, all Angus' difficulties were so minutely described, and his whole case so thoroughly met, that he was filled with surprise; and accepting as of God the counsels that were given him, he finally abandoned, then and there, his intention of joining the Seceders. An attachment was that day formed between him and the minister who preached that sermon that knew no waning while they lived. It was his habit ever after to come occasionally all the way from Auldearn to hear a sermon at Killearnan.

As a speaker, always pointed and lively, Angus never failed to be interesting. His statements of doctrine were always exact, his practical remarks suitable and searching, his reproofs very penetrating, and his counsels specially apt and discriminating. His prayers were very remarkable for childlike freedom and burning earnestness. During thirteen years of his life he enjoyed a continuous assurance of his interest in Christ. Happy were these years spent under the light of his Father's face! Not long before his death the Lord laid His afflicting hand on his body, and withdrew the light of His face from his soul. For a season he walked amidst terrors in "the valley of the shadow of death," but emerging into the light and liberty again, he went singing across the river to the heavenly city.

John Macdonald, Urquhart, was the Turretine of "the men." Trained in early life under a powerful Gospel ministry, his views of the plan of salvation were peculiarly clear. He was intolerant of any deviation from the strictest accuracy in a statement of doctrine, but was intensely practical withal. Often have his luminous and unctuous addresses been blessed "for correction and instruction in righteousness" to the people of God; and not a few received their first impressions of divine things under his teaching. On the Friday of a communion season he was generally the last speaker; and often has he excited the admiration of his hearers by the dexterity with which, after determining the exact state of the question, he would explain or rectify some of the remarks of those who preceded him, and employ for practical uses the bearings of all that had previously been spoken.

"Donald Fraser of the Haugh," as he was called, from the name of the street in Inverness in which he resided, was well known and highly respected. "My minister," he always called Dr Fraser of Kirkhill, for it was under his preaching he was trained in his youth. After the first impression of eternal things was made upon his mind, he was tried with a peculiar temptation. Satan would insist that only great sinners could warrantably expect to be saved, and that as he had been kept from all flagrant transgressions, he ought not to apply for salvation to Christ till he had first qualified himself by committing some crime. Pressed by the tempter, he had almost yielded to his suggestion, when the Lord broke the snare of the fowler. The light of the law's spirituality shed into his soul soon discovered to Donald guilt enough to entitle him to rank with great sinners, without his adding one other to the list of his transgressions. His temptation thereafter was that he was too great a sinner to have any reason to expect that Jesus would receive him. But, on the right hand as on the left, the Lord was near to deliver him, and guided his feet into the way of peace.

One of those who usually spoke at the fellowship meeting in Killearnan in those days was Angus Munro, who retained at fourscore years and five much of the fire of his genius and all the fervour of his love. These righteous ones shall be held in everlasting remembrance. Their several histories shall not be left buried in the dust of the past, but, written on their memories, shall be read over in their heavenly home, to the praise of His wisdom, faithfulness, and love, who kept and guided them by the way. Assembled worlds, too, shall yet hear as much regarding their life on earth proclaimed from the Great White Throne as the glory of their God requires to be made known.

Towards the close of my father's life the only change that could be observed, and that was evident only to a few, was his growing abstraction from the things of time and the increased heavenliness of his doctrine. His bodily health was not impaired, nor was his natural strength abated, and he abounded in labours to the end.

Always deeply interested in all that concerned the welfare of his Church and of his country, he was peculiarly so during the latter years of his life. Being resolutely opposed to Catholic Emancipation, many a groan was wrung from his heart by the Act of 1829. He often referred to it in public, and many incredulously listened to his forebodings of the sad results of that measure. Regarding Papists not merely as the members of the anti-Christian Church, but as the subjects of a foreign prince who aspires to establish as the dominant power in all countries his own temporal as well as spiritual sovereignty, all his loyalty and patriotism, as well as his protestantism, revolted against giving them a place in the legislature. His forebodings were but too well founded; for, whether as the natural result of the increase of its political power, or as a judicial award from the hand of the Highest to the nation that gave so much of its "power to the beast," Popery has since 1829 made greater progress in this country than during the whole century which preceded. The plague of mawkish liberalism which prevailed at the time smote the great majority with blindness as to the true nature and results of the measure, and the few who protested against it were regarded as bigots. Opinion has changed since then; and the concession has lately been wrung from those once loudest in denouncing them that the bigots were right.

The conflict that terminated in the Disruption of the Church of Scotland from the State had been going on for seven years before his death. He never hesitated as to the part he should act in that controversy. On the question of the spiritual independence of the Church he had no difficulty in forming a judgment. The people's right to elect their own pastors he asserted most strongly, but he, at the same time, expressed his fear that they were not qualified to use it. That, however, he did not regard as a reason for retaining it from them; for, as it was given them by Christ, no other power had a right to withhold it. His anticipations of the result of the conflict were very alarming, and to some seemed prophetic. Often did he distinctly announce the event of the Disruption. Dr Macdonald has told me with what surprise he heard him once say, while preaching in the Church of Ferintosh in 1829, "This crowded church shall yet become a place into which none who fear the Lord will dare to enter," adding, "not long before this change shall take place I shall be removed to my rest, but many who now hear me shall see it." From that period till his death, his anticipations were more and more vivid. The coming crisis seemed to emerge, before his eyes, more and more distinctly out of the mist that lay on the future, and that hid its secrets from the eyes of others; and his solicitude, in prospect of the Disruption, wrung more groans from his heart than the actual experience of the trial from the hearts of many who survived it.

His anticipations as to the state of religion in the north during the next generation were extremely gloomy. Often did he declare his persuasion, that the people were wearying of a spiritual ministry, and of a purely-preached Gospel. Like the Israelites in the wilderness, they had begun to count as "light bread" what was sent to them from heaven. "Few and far between" he expected the faithful preachers of the Gospel to be in the generation that succeeded; and when the decay of religion had converted "the garden of the Lord" almost into a wilderness again, he expected a season of trial to come, during which "the man of sin" would again have supremacy, and the witnesses of Christ be few, feeble, and hidden, and through which he could only look with a tearful eye, to the prospect of the glorious Millennium, whose bright morning was seen dawning beyond it.

The religious awakening which, a short time before his death, spread over various districts of Scotland, he did not regard with much hopefulness and pleasure. He expected but little permanent fruit as its result, and was much pained by the countenance given, in the excitement of that time, to manifest delusions. The experience of all his life tended to make him distrustful as to all awakening accompanied with violent bodily excitement, and he never failed to repress any such exhibitions whenever they appeared in his presence. His anticipations were, alas! too fully realised. The rich flush of blossom that then appeared withered prematurely, and almost entirely away, and bitter disappointment awaited those who formed a more sanguine estimate than his of the fruit that might in the end be produced.

Shortly before his death, he took a peculiarly warm interest in the case of a woman in his parish, whom he frequently visited. While engaged with others in planting a piece of moorland, she observed, within the broken walls of a ruined cottage, part of a lady's veil protruding out of a heap of rubbish. Taking hold of it, she was unable to pull it out without removing the stones and turf around it, in doing which a woman's face appeared. The shock caused by this discovery was such that she was almost distracted with terror. The horrid sight of the murdered woman's face — for such it proved to be — was the last her eyes ever saw, for from that moment she was quite blind. Laid aside on a bed of sickness, she remained a helpless invalid till her death. But her reason survived the shock which deprived her of vision, and the Lord visited her with His salvation in the day of her distress. Her pastor's visits were greatly blessed to her, and she was one of the last whom he was the means of turning "from darkness into light." Precious to the blind, as well as to others, were his lectures in her house, and the time spent beside her was to himself a season of peculiar enjoyment. Her Christian course was short, but it seemed to all who knew her to be indeed "the path of the just."

His last pastoral visit was to a pious couple in the east end of his parish, who were apparently dying, and very anxious to see him. The husband was one of his elders, but both in intellect and in spirituality excelled by his wife. Among other questions, he asked them individually, "Do you believe that your affliction was appointed by God in the everlasting covenant?" The wife was first addressed, and her reply was, "I believe that it is permitted by God in His providence, but I have not attained to believe that it was ordered in the covenant." The husband's answer was, "I cannot even say what my wife has just said." "You are a step behind her, Donald," his minister said, "and as surely as she is before you in this, she will be before you in heaven." And so it happened; though the husband was both older, and a greater invalid than his wife.

After leaving this house he passed into the parish of Knockbain, to visit a woman who had been for many years one of his stated hearers, and whose soul had profited by his preaching. She was enduring great agony under the gnawing of a virulent cancer, and her soul's hope was, at the same time, sorely tried by the tempter. Her case had for some time lain closely on his heart, and his frequent and earnest references to her in family prayers indicated how intensely he desired her deliverance from her deep despondency. Much of his interview with her was strictly private. Its result was her complete deliverance from the fetters in which Satan, for a season, bound her. She was enabled, ere they parted, to declare her assurance of salvation, her contentment with her lot, and her willingness to leave the event of her death in the good hand of Him to whom she had committed her spirit. Her eyes were moist with tears, but her face was bright with joy, as she bade him farewell; and, before a fortnight passed, they met, for the next time, in their eternal home in heaven.

His references to his death were frequent in his preaching during the last year of his life, and his appeals to his hearers were peculiarly earnest and solemn. His anticipation of death was so assured, that he could not refrain from referring to it, and he himself preparing, he desired to prepare his people also, for the parting which drew near. He would announce the subject of a course of sermons, and open it up; but, instead of resuming it next Sabbath, he would mention a new text. This again would be laid aside for another. He was thus hurried over a series of texts in such pressing haste that he could not but direct the attention of his people to the fact, entreating them to observe how his Master was urging him to fulfil his ministry with all haste, as the end of it was near. One of his last Sabbath texts was Rev. 3: 20. His sermons on that verse were very remarkable, and were indeed like the utterances of one who was just going to step across the threshold of eternity.

For a few weeks before his death he preached every Tuesday evening from the words, ''We are come to God, the Judge of all.'' This text was the announcement of his death to his people, and his sermons contained much of his own feeling in prospect of that event. His last sermon in church was preached on the Tuesday evening before his death, and it closed the series of discourses on the text last mentioned. At the close of the service he announced that on Thursday he would preach in the schoolhouse in the eastern district of the parish in order to take that last opportunity of wiping off his skirts the blood of the people who resided there. The congregation was then dismissed by him under the assured persuasion that he and they would never meet again on earth. On coming out of church he stood for a few minutes looking to the people as they were retiring under the clear moonlight. ''My poor people,'' he was heard exclaiming by one who had come up beside him, and whose approach caused him to turn away, and to hurry on to the Manse.

All this time he was in perfect health, his step almost as firm and elastic as when he was in the prime of his manhood. The usual indications of approaching dissolution were entirely awanting, and yet his persuasion of death being nigh was quite assured. His sermon on Thursday was on spiritual worship, and in preaching it his whole soul seemed to go out in aspirations after the pure service of heaven. On Friday his throat became affected. Inflammation set in, and continued to make progress. He expressed no anxiety, and uttered no complaint, and his family had no distinct anticipation of danger. Remaining in bed, he seemed lost in contemplation, an expression of placid joy resting on his face. He had calmly laid himself down to die. His work was done, he knew that his eternal rest was nigh; and with his eye fixed on the glory that was dawning on his vision, he awaited with joyful expectation the coming of death. His reply to all enquiries about his health was, ''I'll soon be quite well.'' While his wife and a pious friend were sitting in his room, not till then excited by alarm as to the issue of his illness, their attention was suddenly arrested by sounds of the sweetest melody. Such was the softness of the strange music, they felt as if it could not have been a thing of earth, and while it lasted they could only listen in solemn silence. When the spell was broken, Mrs Kennedy hastened to ask him if he had heard any strange music. He gave no answer, but beckoned her to be silent, with an expression of absorbed attention and of ecstacy on his face. Her rising fears then

Appendix

THE SECRET OF THE LORD

"The secret of the Lord is with them that fear Him."
Psalm 25. 14.

A LL true Christians are peculiar. Their singular character and
their exclusive privileges make them so. The Lord causes them
to differ from all others by what He does in them, and by what He
does for them. He creates a new heart in them, and they fear Him.
He puts His spirit within them, and makes known to them His
mind. Into their soul He infuses life, and into their ear He speaks
His secrets. Fearers of God are thus favourites of God; and both as
His fearers and His favourites they are a peculiar people.

I. True Christians differ from all others because they only fear
the Lord. "I will put my fear within them" is a promise fulfilled to
them all, and to them only. Covenant grace was put within them
ere covenant secrets were made known unto them.

Those who fear the Lord are, and must be, quickened souls. They
were once dead in sins, but they are now alive to God; and they live
because they were "quickened together with Christ." The fear of
God in them is just the life of God in them suitably responding to
the manifestation of "the glory of God in the face of Jesus Christ."
These realise God as others do not. They know Him as none else do
know Him. They alone approve of His character and appreciate His
greatness. There are Godward movements in their hearts as in no
hearts besides. Of them only does the Lord say, "they shall not
depart from me."

A soul, spiritually dead, may be moved by an enslaving dread of
God; but there can be no Godward advances in such a case. Farther
and farther from God will that soul depart, who, left unrenewed,
feels the terrors of His wrath. What causes his fear inflames his
enmity. The more helpless he feels before the fire of God's anger,

the more active is his enmity before the brightness of God's purity. Fearing and hating Him at once, the unquickened soul departeth from the living God.

Those who fear, must be near to, God. They were once "far off," but they have been brought nigh by the blood of Jesus. In the covenant right of Jesus the quickening spirit came to them when they were far off and dead. He caused them to live, and He united them to Christ. Being clothed in the righteousness of Christ they were justified by God; the criminals were pardoned and made heirs of life; and they received power to become the sons of God. Having a right to communion with God, the Spirit guides them to the throne of grace. Their homage at the footstool of that throne is fear. It is neither the rebel, who dreads the king's approach, as he skulks on the outskirts of the kingdom, nor the stranger, who has never visited the sovereign, who can do him homage in loyal friendly deference to his rank and rule; but the courtier or the child, who is in the palace and in the presence of the king. So only those who are His loving children and His loyal servants, can honour the Lord as a father, and as a master fear Him.

In their approaches to God on His throne of grace, they mingle reverence of His glory with hope in His mercy. This is a combination only found where the true fear of God is. Others may have either a slavish fear without hope, or a presumptuous hope without fear; but the view of God which inspires hope in the heart of a Christian produces also reverential fear. The glory of God, as seen in the cross, commands his admiration as well as his trust. It is at once solemnising and encouraging. It bears him down while it draws him near. It breaks his heart as surely as it cheers it. And the more it has of the one effect the more it has of the other. The more clearly he discerns the rigour of divine righteousness and the steadfastness of divine truth, the more he is constrained to reverence and encouraged to hope. It is to the mercy that is accompanied with truth he humbly ventures to appeal, and he can claim peace, only when he sees it in the embrace of righteousness. His confidence increases with his admiration of God's character and his awe of His majesty. His fear is not now in conflict with his hope. Solemn awe only gives zest to his enjoyment of liberty in the presence of God. The more I am persuaded that it is the sovereign with whom I commune, the more I prize the tokens of that sovereign's favour. I may, perhaps, have met him on a journey divested of the insignia of royalty. I may then have received some token of favour, but it cheered me not as it would if I had gotten it from the king, when wearing his crown and seated on his throne amidst the splendour of his court. What proved him king and glorious would make me all the more prize his favour. I might have feared that it was not as king that he was my friend before, and that he would not acknowledge in open court the poor man to whom he then happened to be kind. But when from the very throne he helps me, how precious is his kindness and how cheering to my heart! I cared not so much for his kindness, nor would I so depend upon it, when I could stand up before him as he showed me favour. But how invaluable do I reckon his condescension when I can only receive the token of it lying prostrate at His footstool!

They who fear the Lord seek to do His will. He who does homage to the Lord at the footstool of His throne comes forth to serve Him. In earthly families there are children who make a show of affection in their manner towards their father, but quite forget to do his will when he is out of sight. There are no such children in the heavenly family. Men have children who cannot refrain from expressing a reverent love to their fathers when they are near them, and who act according to their directions when they send them on an errand. Such as these do all God's children seek to be. But in human families are sometimes found children who have not courage to use filial liberty with their father when they are near him, but who prove themselves to be children indeed by their endeavours to please him. They cannot claim the child's privilege, but they do the child's work. They do not commune as children, but they obey as children. There are some such in the family of God.

They have respect to all their Father's commandments. They do not, like the Pharisees, pick out those to which they find it most convenient to have respect, and leave the rest. Their righteousness exceedeth in *breadth* "the righteousness of Scribes and Pharisees." Nor do they rest contented unless their obedience arises from the heart; they seek to obey out of genuine love. Their righteousness thus exceeds in *depth* "the righteousness of Scribes and Pharisees." The aim of their service is higher; they "seek" not "their own," but "the things which are Jesus Christ's." That the Lord may be pleased and glorified is the end to which they aspire. Their righteousness thus exceeds in *height* "the righteousness of Scribes and Pharisees." Matthew 5: 20.

Their right to privileges depends not at all, but their enjoyment of privileges depends greatly, on their obedience. They cannot be happy without having respect to all God's commandments. Psalm 119: 6. They must first seek grace to fear the Lord in order that His secret may be with them. When they wander from His way, He will either frown upon them and be silent, or He will frown upon them and rebuke them with stern words, or He will frown upon them and chasten them with His rod. They shall not be cast out of their father's house because they sin; but when they "regard iniquity in" their "heart the Lord will not hear" them. Psalm 66: 18. When they have departed from the Lord they shall not again enjoy the light of His face till their backslidings have been healed. Isaiah 57: 18. An offended father may thrust out his child from his presence, and that child may for a time be outside with the dogs, but he is a child there as surely as when he lay on his father's bosom. He has not been thrust out of the Father's heart nor has he finally forfeited his place in the Father's house. Till the Lord shall "utterly take" His "loving kindness from him" who is the Elder Brother, He will not disown the adopted sons whom "the Only Begotten" has made free. He abideth in the house for ever, and so shall they. Psalm 89: 30-34; John 8: 35-36.

It is just, then, as the life of God in their souls is exercised in seeking their Father's face and strength, and they through grace endeavour to do His will, that those who fear the Lord may expect His secret to be with them.

II. True Christians differ from all others, because with them only is "the secret of the Lord." "The secret" which is with them is hidden in the mind of God from all to whom He does not reveal it. "Thou hast hid these things," saith Jesus to the Father, "from the wise and prudent, and has revealed them unto babes." Matthew 11: 25.

This surely means more than that they have the Bible in their hands. True, in it, there is a complete revelation of the will of God. It is by it, too, that God communicates all the knowledge of His mind to which men shall attain on earth. But many have the Bible in whom the fear to the Lord is not found, and to whom the secret of the Lord is not given. They who fear the Lord have received, not the spirit of the world, but the Spirit which is of God, that "they might know the things that are freely given to" them "of God." It is thus that they are "made to differ."

"He will manifest to them His covenant." This covenant — the covenant of grace — was once known only to God himself. It was then written only in the volume of the book which contained a record of the eternal counsels of the Godhead, and on which no eye looked but that of God himself. But He gradually revealed the plan and provision of that covenant, when the earth was formed, and men were, and were sinners, on it. The revelation of that covenant, intended for men on earth, is now complete. A clearer light from heaven shall never shine on earth than that which now illumines these last Gospel days. "The word of the Lord," as it now is, "abideth for ever." But not only does the Lord shine with Gospel light on them that fear Him, as He does on all around them; He hath also shined into their hearts, giving them the light of the knowledge of His glory in the face of Jesus Christ. 2 Cor. 4: 6. He has taught to them their need of the grace of the everlasting covenant. He has made known to them its plan and its provision. They, and only they, have "tasted that the Lord is gracious." But they know only a very little. They need that He would still continue to manifest His covenant unto them. And He will do so. Into all truth the Spirit of God shall guide them. All the lessons appointed by their Father shall be learned by them; and all their darkness and folly shall, at the last, be utterly removed. John 16: 13.

The Spirit, who makes known and applies the provision of the covenant, and who, in doing so, first quickeneth the dead, hath given unto these the peculiar knowledge which they have. Their knowledge, therefore, is spiritual; not merely because the Spirit gave it, but because they were made spiritual in order to receive it. It is the spirit born of the Spirit that takes knowledge of the things of God. It is the life of God in their understanding that perceives the mind of God in His Word. That same life in the heart seeks the enjoyment of what is known. This desire accords with God's gracious design; for His people have been enlightened to know, just in order to partake of the things of God. They are, therefore, helped to receive them by faith. And their faith is not exercised in vain. The fulness of covenant grace in Christ is reached and communicated, and out of that fulness they receive, "and grace for grace." John 1: 16. As the High Priest in heaven pleads, "Sanctify them through thy truth," so, under His government and by His Spirit, they on the earth receive; and "beholding as in a glass the glory of the Lord," they "are changed into the same image, from glory to glory, even as by the Spirit of the Lord." 2 Cor. 4: 18.

But is there nothing more intimate than this in God's intercourse with His people? Is this all that is implied in the secret of the Lord being with them that fear Him? Is this peculiar privilege exhausted in their receiving a saving knowledge of the covenant of grace as revealed in the gospel? Is this all the proof given of their being the favourites of heaven? Is it what is barely necessary for their salvation alone God gives to His beloved people? Giveth He no assurance to them of His love to themselves individually? Do they remain ignorant of His mind in reference to the cases which they carry to His footstool, and there spread out before Him? Is God silent when they plead for others? Does he altogether hide from them, as he does from the world, the bearings and coming issues of His providence? Surely they are deceived who think that these things are so. And yet how many there are who would evacuate the communion of the Lord with His people of all special proofs of how near and dear to Him they are, and who regard the privilege, referred to in the text, as enjoyed merely in the attainment of what is essential to salvation.

It is one extreme statement that God reveals aught to His people apart from the Bible, but it is another that He makes known to them only what is there directly revealed. We must not expect to know the mind of God but by means of the written word. ''The law and the testimony'' must be our only guide in knowing, our only standard in judging of ''the things of God.'' To that light must we repair to examine what is of God, and to that rule to try what professes to be of Him. Isa. 8: 19, 20. But surely God does not make known to His people what is not directly revealed in His word; although He does not do so except by means of what is written.

He often maketh known their election to them who fear him. He acquaints them with His everlasting purpose to save them; yet this is not directly revealed. The fact of the election of any particular individual is not found written in the Bible; and yet by means of the word in connection with His work of grace, He, by His Spirit, maketh it known to believers. The secret of His everlasting purpose of mercy is thus with them that fear Him. Of His special covenant love to themselves individually they are made assured, but in a manner very different from that in which they are persuaded of His ''good will to men.'' Tokens of that love the Lord giveth to His people; but his way of doing so is a secret hid from all who do not receive them.

Thus, too, by means of the written word, does God often reveal to them who fear Him the issues to which He will bring their cases when they deal with Him by prayer. Applying to their case ''a word in season,'' He excites an expectation of such a result as that word doth indicate, and thus His purpose of dealing with them in a particular way is made known. They are thus enabled to anticipate an event in their own spiritual history, without receiving any revelation of God's unfulfilled purposes apart from the light of Scripture.

A mere outside Christian is an utter stranger to any such intimations of the Lord's will by the special application of the statements or promises of the Bible. He judges that communion with the Lord is a one-sided matter. He thinks that in dealing with the Hearer of prayer the speaking is all on his own side. He is so enamoured of his own utterances that he cares not whether God speaks or not. But it is far otherwise with those who truly fear the Lord. It is when they hear the Lord's voice speaking words of truth and mercy that they can venture to utter words of faith and hope. "Take not the word of truth utterly out of my mouth; for I have hoped in thy judgments." "Cause me to hear thy loving-kindness in the morning; for in thee do I trust." "Be not silent to me." "The companions hearken to thy voice; cause me to hear it." There are times when, in the face of His silence, as surely as in the face of His frown, they who fear Him cannot advance nor speak to the Lord. And when they have presented their suit, they look up for an answer in peace. This, in the meantime, the Lord often gives them by "a word in season" spoken to their heart. It may, sometimes, please Him not to give any intimation of His acceptance of their prayer till the time for granting their request has come. But it is not always so. Many seem to think that all that is allowed to petitioners at the footstool of mercy, at any time, is liberty to hope because of God's character and His general promises of grace; and that they must wait, without any more special encouragement, till the course of providence has borne to them an answer to their cry.

"The secret of the Lord is with them that fear Him," *as to the cases of others, for whom they plead.* The Spirit of prayer may suggest, and often does, the case of a particular individual, to the mind of one who is pleading at the footstool of mercy. With the suggested case may come a suggested portion of Scripture. In the light of the latter, the former is considered; and, as thus seen, is laid before the Lord. To the case thus presented, the Lord may apply a passage of Scripture to indicate His mind regarding it, and to give to the pleader a favourable or unfavourable anticipation of the result. That premonition may be more or less distinct; but, even when assuring, it is something very different from the inspiration of the prophet. It results entirely from an adaptation by God Himself of His own written word.

They who fear the Lord are not blind, as others are, to the indications of His mind in the dealings of His providence. They are acquainted, as others are not, with the principles of His moral government. They have the sensitiveness of spiritual life under the workings of His great hand, while others lie unaffected in death. They watch and walk with God, while others live without Him in the world. They speak to Him about His doings, and He speaks to them, while others are dumb and deaf before Him. Shall they not therefore know the bearings of God's providence, as others cannot? May not one, who fears the Lord, who is much given unto prayer, whose heart is charged with care about the interests of the cause of Christ, who watches over the movements of providence with a feeling of intensest interest, who looks on God's works in the light of His word, and of His recorded antecedents, and who has acquired the blessed habit of speaking about His doings to the Lord Himself, seem to penetrate a future, all dark to others, as with a seer's eye, while, with all truth and honesty, he may disclaim being either a prophet or the son of one? "They are little acquainted with the ways of God," says the godly and judicious Dr Love, "who imagine God has ceased to give His people assurance as to future events. God has not bound Himself in this manner; and there have been many things intimated to, and known by the most eminent saints, before such things came to pass."

It is well to mark the difference between the knowledge derived from the direct teaching of the Bible, and that which is only indirectly obtained by means of it. It were a great mistake to attribute equal certainty to the information received in each of these ways. In the former case, the intelligence comes to me directly, and lies before me plainly written in the Word of God. And is it not well that it is the knowledge which is "life eternal" that is thus obtained? In order to "believe to the saving of the soul," I must know Him in whom salvation is to be found, the terms on which His salvation is bestowed, and the warrant given me by God for casting my lost soul into the hands of "His anointed." And all this is clearly and directly revealed. In times of doubting, the Christian can repair to the Bible, and find, plainly written there, what he requires to know regarding the object and warrant of his faith.

But his own personal interest in Christ is not matter of direct revelation. In acquiring information regarding this, much depends upon the mode of God's dealing with his soul. The fruit of God's secret work, as well as the matter of His open revelation, must be taken into account in seeking information of his being a child of God. He is sometimes so assured of this as to be free from all doubting regarding it; but never is his hope of this so fixed and unvarying as his persuasion of God's goodwill to him as a sinner.

More uncertain is his knowledge of God's mind regarding the cases which he brings to the mercy-seat. All depends here on the special application of the truth being verily by God. What is plainly written in the Bible I know to be of God. But I have not the same ground for saying that the suggestion to my mind, and the application to my case, of what is written, is of God; and on these depends the goodness of the information, which, in this instance, I think I possess regarding the mind of the Lord. Verily the Lord can give an assurance of this. He can so impress a soul with His authority. He may so disclose the treasures of His grace, and may so help one to appropriate what the word conveys to him, that there is no room left for doubting. But the man cannot fall back on this again, when misgivings arise, as he can on the direct teaching of Scripture regarding the way of salvation. So much depends, in the former case, on his own discernment, on his spirituality of mind, on his nearness to God, and on his sensitiveness to God's dealings with his soul, that he feels a vast difference between the hope of everlasting salvation, founded on the call of the Gospel, and the hope of a particular result in this life, founded on a word of promise, which seemed to have come from the Lord.

Still greater is the uncertainty of the information which he thinks the Lord has given him, regarding the prospects of others for whom he was pleading in prayer. He cannot, in this case, claim, as a promise given to himself in Christ, the word which has been suggested to his mind. He cannot now, when afraid to receive the word as from God, fall back on his warrant to receive Christ, and embracing Him anew in Gospel offer, approach, on the ground of His right, to the grace of the promise suggested to his mind. His information depending, as it is, on his own spiritual sensitiveness and discernment, partakes of the comparative uncertainty that attaches to all that is subjective.

And greater still is the uncertainty of the information which guides him in anticipating a certain result from a course of providence. Even in the case of those grand results that are indicated in the unfulfilled prophecies of the Bible, and which form the great landmarks of the future, how uncertain is the light in which he tries to forecast them. And when examining providences on which the light of prophecy does not shine, while he is so dependent for any just anticipation on his own spirituality of mind, his nearness to God, and his ability to discern the mind of God in the word which is suggested to explain the doings of His hand, how far removed from the certainty of his knowledge, regarding what is essential to salvation, is any information, regarding the future, which he may think he possesses.

But while this is true, it is quite as true that, in all the ways that have been indicated, ''the secret of the Lord'' may be ''with them that fear Him.'' 'And let us not limit the Holy One, as if He were not able, in all these instances, to give infallible direction and ''much assurance.'' The comparative uncertainty of the information in some of these is altogether due to the subjectiveness of the mode in which it is obtained. It is in these cases, therefore, that the truth of the text is most manifestly proved. It is in connection with them the Christian most thoroughly realizes that, in order to know ''the secret of the Lord,'' he must be ''of quick understanding in the fear of the Lord.''

It is not difficult to find the reason why those, who are themselves strangers to communion with God, are so ready to denounce as superstition all faith in the reality of information from heaven, besides that which is given in the direct teachings of Scripture. They cannot bear to think that those who fear the Lord have reached any attainment beyond themselves, and to which, by any amount of painstaking, they cannot advance. This wounds their pride, and tends to make them uneasy in their alienation from God. They may allow that unusual knowledge is attained by those who are ''disciples indeed,'' from the direct teaching of Scripture, for this they can hope to imitate. Their own unsanctified knowledge of what is written they can make to appear, to themselves at least, not unlike to what these have obtained immediately from the pages of Scripture. They could hold up their heads among the godly if this were all their attainment. The most convenient way of getting rid of their uneasiness is to regard as superstitious the attainment that is beyond them. They can make out a case, with a plausible surface, in support of their opinion.

"It is pretending to know," they say, "what is not revealed in Scripture." This sounds well. It seems, at first sight, due to the Word of God, as the only complete revelation of His will, that we should at once regard as false all information regarding the mind of God not derived directly from the plain import of Scripture. They have never gone beneath the surface in their thinking on this matter, who have not discovered the extremeness of this view. But, backed by this false assumption, some will quote, with an air of triumph, the pretensions to inspiration, the claims of the gift of prophecy, the faith in dreams and visions, of those whom all acknowledge to have been deceivers and deceived. To minds that have always kept far off from the realities of a life of godliness, that look from a distance on the communion of His people with the Lord, the difference between the baseless pretensions of deceivers and the God-given privilege of the righteous is utterly impalpable. All kinds of intercourse with the Invisible are classed by these together, and to them all who claim the privilege of communion with the Lord appear as deluded fanatics. More triumphant still is their air, when they can quote, in support of their position, the mistakes of those who were truly godly. But, surely, it is not difficult to discover a very good reason why the Lord should allow even these to be sometimes deceived in their anticipations, and in their readings of the page of Providence. Such mistakes only prove that they are always prone to error, when the correctness of their information specially depends upon their own spirituality. They need to learn this, and their falls will teach them. And their painful experience of their proneness to wander here, will help to make all the more precious to them the certainty attaching to what is the standing ground of their hope — a plain "thus saith the Lord," on some page of Scripture.

1. Let none forget that "the secret of the Lord is" *only* "with them that fear Him." Let no one dare to claim the privilege of having "the secret of the Lord" who seeks not to walk in His fear. Of all pretensions this is the vilest. While disregarding the Lord's claims to our homage it is impious to claim His secret. It is sacrilege to lay a dishonest hand on the peculiar privileges of His people; and it is daring hypocrisy to deck oneself with a counterfeit of these before the eyes of men, and to walk in pride under this disguise, beneath the gaze of the Omniscient, who, looking down from heaven, sees within a heart that is an utter stranger to His fear.

There is something, in the more peculiar attainments of the righteous, which excites an unholy and dishonest ambition in those who seek "the honour that cometh from man." Men have pretended to know, as others knew not, the mind of the Lord, who exhibited no such difference, between themselves and the world, as there is "between him that feareth God and him that feareth Him not." When out of sight they have pretended to be holding converse with God, but their faces did not shine when they came down from the mount. But "from him that hath not" the true fear of the Lord "shall be taken even that which he seemeth to have." The wise course is to seek to have the fear of God within us, to pray for grace to keep that fear in exercise, and to leave in the hands of Him, who divideth "to every man severally as He will," to determine to what extent "the secret of the Lord" shall be with us.

2. Let none of the Lord's people settle down into formality in their intercourse with God on the foregone conclusion, that it is not legitimate to seek, with deference to the Divine sovereignty, the more peculiar attainments to which reference has been made. The time was, when, during a close walk with God, some of His people enjoyed such nearness to Him, that it would have surprised them if they received no token of His favour whenever they bowed themselves in prayer before Him; if they were overtaken by a trial, of which, through the Word, they had no previous intimation; and if a brother or sister were in trouble, and they found not their case on

their spirits. But there is now a change. They have backslidden from the Lord. They hear not His voice now, as in other and better days. They are becoming content without any such tokens of His love as once were given them. They are beginning to be satisfied with a peradventure as to their interest in Christ. They are inclining to think that, beyond the vague encouragement derived from the general tenor of the Gospel, and the aspect of God's character as therein revealed, they ought not, as they care not, to seek any more definite and personal intimation of His favour. Or they have learned to handle, in cold easy formality, the precious promises of grace, without caring to taste their sweetness or to feel their power. The liberty and songs of their youth are now no longer theirs; nor will they recover them till their backslidings are healed. Hos. 2: 15. The fear of the Lord must be revived within them ere His secret shall again be with them.

3. Let all beware of an unlawful employment of the Word of God, as well as of entire ignorance of its sweetness and its power. There are who find it easy to appropriate to themselves without misgiving the precious promises of the Word, not caring to ascertain their right to them in Christ, to be rightly informed of the mind of God as expressed in them, or to be strengthened to take hold of the truth and power and grace of Him who gave them at His footstool. There are others who lay themselves open to the suggestion of ''a word'' as they crave encouragement or direction; and who, if a Scripture saying which seems seasonable comes abruptly into their mind, conclude, because of its suitableness and suddenness, that it is a message to them from heaven. These care not whether their application of it accords with the scope of the passage in which it occcurs; they realise not His authority whose Word it is; and they desiderate no experience of its sanctifying power. It is convenient for them to get it, and it seems to them safe to take it, and this is all about which they care.

There are others still who have settled down in the conviction that a speculative acquaintance with what is written is all that it is wise to seek. Utter strangers to the seasonable suggestion of the truth by the Lord, blind to the wonders of grace which the world unfolds, without any exercise of appropriating faith in Christ whom it reveals, and destitute of all experience of its power to kill or to quicken, to wound or to heal, to cast down or to raise up, to burn as a fire or to break as a hammmer — these go on at their ease, without joy in the communion, or profit from the Word of the Lord.

But let it be ours to be dependent on the gracious and effectual teaching of the Spirit of truth, under whose guidance even fools can be kept from wandering, and who can make it impossible that even they can be deceived. Let us not think that, amidst the multiform delusion which prevaileth, there is no genuineness and no security. They are a people who have an unction from the Holy One, and who know all things. These have genuine wisdom, and they have good security from error. Let us seek to have fellowship with them. Let us not be content with what is barely necessary to salvation in our intercourse with God. From unholy aspirations after being like the Christian in some of his attainments, without being like him in his character, may the Lord deliver us. May we be kept athirst for communion with the Lord, and seeking grace to prepare us to enjoy it. Let His Word be precious to us, and may we be wise to use it for the ends for which it is given. Let us aspire after clearer views of its wonders, a simpler faith in its truth, a more ravishing sense of its sweetness, and a deeper experience of its power. And thus may we be guided by its light, moulded by its form, fed by its manna, and cheered by its comforts, ''until the day dawn, and the day star arise in our hearts''; till perfect likeness to Christ is attained; till the land of promise and of plenty is reached, and the fulness of pleasures enjoyed, at the right hand of God.